EDUCATION AND THE
PERSONAL QUEST

STUDIES OF THE PERSON

edited by

Carl R. Rogers
William R. Coulson

EDUCATION AND THE PERSONAL QUEST

Lloyd W. Kline

University of Massachusetts

CHARLES E. MERRILL PUBLISHING COMPANY

A Bell and Howell Company Columbus, Ohio

International Standard Book Number: 0-675-09195-0

Library of Congress Catalog Card Number: 76-163442

1 2 3 4 5 6 7 8 9 10 / 75 74 73 72 71

PRINTED IN THE UNITED STATES OF AMERICA

EDITORS' NOTE

We are very happy to welcome this volume into the Series, Studies of the Person. We are particularly appreciative of the perceptive Foreword, giving a vision of education's future, by Dean Dwight W. Allen, himself a dynamic and powerful innovator in the field of teacher training. We believe this book provides a new and very valuable perspective for educators.

Carl R. Rogers
William R. Coulson

Center for Studies of the Person
La Jolla, California

FOREWORD

By DWIGHT W. ALLEN
Dean, School of Education
University of Massachusetts

The twentieth century may be remembered in history as the dawn of the triumph of the person—the time when the preoccupation of education changed from man's relationship to things to man's relationship to man, perhaps in terms of my own personal bias anticipating a concern with man's relationship to the ultimate destiny of the individual and the world.

But, at this moment in history, such a statement is still a matter of conjecture, for dramatic changes in emphasis will be required before education can truly be deemed oriented to the individual and his interface with the world around him. In such an educational system we will study scientific, political, and historical subsystems as they relate to man's interface with his present and future environment, primarily his human environment. We will mold an educational system that is sensitive to man's use of resources for human purposes, where projections and predictions will reflect the complexities of human interaction and be seen not simply as cumulative effects but as geometric ratios impartially projecting the good or evil of the world, depending upon the leverage and direction that we can bring to bear in our early encounters.

Many authors have attempted to deal with developing individually human potential. This volume offers a model that, in my opinion, is more promising than most—eclectic in the sense that it seeks to find ways to appreciate and use the differences that usually stand between the humanist and the scientist. Rather than forcing the two positions into a common mold, however, it aims for a coexistence, for a merging of appreciation rather than tolerance. This blending is all the more

vii

noteworthy because of Lloyd Kline's personal humanistic biases, which the hardnosed scientific researcher will undoubtedly be tempted to cite as the reason for dismissing much of the claim advanced by this author. Yet, that same scientist no doubt has found himself joined in equal measures of anger by humanists who feel that there can be no compromise with the dehumanizing compulsions of technology and its artificial, nonhuman priorities of efficiency and interchangeability. Both are wrong, of course, for ultimately technology must be seen as a force to humanize education, and humanistic concerns must embrace the indispensable nature of technological allies if the human potential is to be freed from mundane preoccupations with survival and creature comfort.

Such a blend has an impact on education in two ways. First, it encourages redefinition of the goals of education and the institutional frameworks within which such goals are pursued. More important, it pushes us to examine the methodology, the arbitrary and conventional wisdom of prerequisites, linear learning, extravagant commitment to memory learning, conversion answers to standard and preemptive questions. In short, it seeks ways to shape institutions to serve individuals.

We must find ways to reward the fuzzy romantic, the narrow technologist, the eclectic, the visionary, the architect, the executor, the landscapers of human design. Somehow education must find ways to examine its own directions, to quest after unity and diversity simultaneously, to ask rather than answer. This volume furthers earlier statements of such human concern within formal education. It succeeds in avoiding at least some of the neo-orthodoxies that belabor many attempts at innovation and change. Hopefully, such concern and such success will lead only to renewed innovation, or at least to yet another fresh view for all to try through yet another man's perspective.

ACKNOWLEDGMENTS

The book that follows is so personal that to begin listing those people I have known over the years to whom either thanks or apologies are due would be to produce a second version of the book. There are those who populate the various anecdotes carried in the book, and those who stand in my memory and experience just behind every line that I have written. There are those who have encouraged me in the various beliefs and projects that have culminated in this book, and those who have admonished me against developing and publishing elements of it. There are those who have served as critical readers for materials in manuscript form, and those who have encountered or persevered the oral barrage of many conversations. There is the class that first worked through the "poetics of education" with me. There are family and friends who have suffered my short temper or ill attention yet supported my various efforts and idiosyncracies in countless ways. There are neighbors who have survived the noise of the typewriter at odd hours and in what sometimes must have seemed endless session. To all of them, warmer thanks than I could ever convey by listing their names in a preface.

If I had not met Dean Dwight Allen, I would not have found the year at the University of Massachusetts during which this volume largely got committed to paper. I thank him here by name—both for that year and for a thousand other reasons that most general readers would not believe even if they understood.

The names of most people mentioned in the volume that follows have been changed from their originals, usually to avoid any unnecessary embarrassment to anyone.

Lloyd W. Kline

They would not find me changed from him they knew—
Only more sure of all I thought was true.

Robert Frost

CONTENTS

I

Anger—Wellspring of Inquiry

One of the interesting facts about my brief study of Latin many years ago in my high school curriculum is that I learned something that has haunted me ever since and that what I learned is not exactly what the teacher was teaching.

No, I am not referring to the cliché that "Latin is not a dead language but a living language." What a fallacious distortion of the concept of "dead language" lies behind that one.

And, no, I am not punning with the word *haunted*, although Latin conjugations and declensions, as items immediately relevant to our punky little lives, did not have a ghost of a chance, to quote the title of a song popular during my high school days, a song to which we very relevantly held our blossoming adolescent girl-friends close to us as we scuffled around a dance floor.

And, no, I am not referring to the fact that every time I look at a U.S. coin, I recall one of the few points that I can of the many that my Latin teacher must have made: *E Pluribus Unum* means *one from many*, although the Romans would not have capitalized it (I also recall) for some reason unexplained to us ninth graders.

What I learned—and the teacher is chiefly responsible for opening me up to the first part of it—is the phenomenon of derivation, which led me to amateur and often whimsical etymology in my spare moments in school. In other words, when I was bored with whatever was being taught and even when I was simply in my natural state—alone and learning out there in the real world away from school—I took an inside look at the Latin words and at the English words borrowed from Latin that seemed to fill so many blackboards in school. These words more often than not were called "Vocabulary Lists," and they seemed foreign enough, especially in our English classes. There were words like *expedite, mortify, corpulent, homicidal.* The words in our own real world as adolescents were racy little items like *jive, hep cat, swing, bebop,*

3

zoot suit, man alive, plus a most astounding array of utterances usually labelled as profanity or obscenity and completely non-existent, we assumed, to school people. Or, in the real world of home and church, there were words like *God, sin, world, love, forever and ever,* and *amen*—quiet, thoughtful, awesome words. But *expedite, mortify,* and company—they belonged in school.

That is, until I introduced myself to the fine art of amateur etymology: how to psych out a borrowed word in our language.

Take *expedite,* for instance—a Latinate if ever there was one. It appeared on one Vocabulary List or another, and we memorized one synonym or another for it from the dictionary, synonyms equally familiar to it in our jivey, adolescent, post-World War II-ish lives: *facilitate, accelerate, dispatch,* and the like. And we passed the regular vocabulary test by dutifully penning such equally familiar synonyms on our quiz papers. Meanwhile, I put the word to a vocabulary test of my own. "*Ex ped ite.* Hmm, literally from the Latin, '*off* or *from* the *foot*'. How about '*kick it off*'? The board of commissioners decided to expedite the matter —in other words, kick it off to a good start." Not bad. I had taken language from their world, brought it into our kind of language, and bridged some kind of gap. Might I by similar process take some of our world into theirs by reversing the language from slang to Latinate rather than from Latinate to slang? Wouldn't it be funny, for instance, to say to my buddy, "*Get your ass off my bicycle, or I shall posthaste expedite it* (kick it off) *for you*"?

Of course, such thinking got you nowhere in school. It might draw a few chuckles from the less thickheaded of your buddies, but it would bring nary a smile from the school people. School just ain't no place for no kind of fun—certainly not intelligent or creative fun. And we all recognized that the word *ass* did not exist for school people at any rate, except in the parable of the Good Samaritan (in certain translations) and a few other selected passages from Scripture that we occasionally heard during "Daily Opening Exercises." Furthermore, *kick it off* was one of our phrases, used out there in the real world. Just dare suggest to the teacher that *kick it off* might serve as a fitting definition of *expedite* on your vocabulary test. If conservative, she would throw you out of class for rudeness. If moderate, she might let you off merely by reading your response to the class and calling down appropriate gales of ridicule to be heaped upon your little adventure into amateur etymology. If liberal, she might simply utter a private revulsion as she read your paper but give you credit for having tried, especially if she were in one of her more benevolent moods toward your pitiful and hopeless condition as scholar.

Still, my amateur etymology persisted as a clandestine enterprise and has come with me to this very day. *Mortify* means more to me if I imagine some Roman matron confiding to her friend, "I could have died (from Latin *mors, mortis,* death) when my husband's toga fell off—right there in the Coliseum entrance!" *Corpulent* carries more weight with me (forgive that pun) whenever I see a mound of flesh waddling along the beach and think to myself, "Man, what a lot of body (from Latin *corpus,* body) to lug around with you." *Homicidal* (from Latin *homo,* man, and *caedo,* to kill or to cut) picks up all kinds of relevance for me, especially as in *homicidal tendencies,* whenever I hear someone say, "Oh, boy, did she cut him dead after that remark!" (I assume that Romans more often than not cut their man whenever they wanted to kill him since daggers, swords, and spears had replaced or at least supplemented clubs at that high stage of civilization.)

So, this fancy of mine for amateur etymology led eventually toward a linguistic hypothesis that I mean to test out someday, if ever I decide to play school as so many traditional schoolmen would have me play it—by becoming a bookish scholar. The hypothesis is rather simply stated: Slang might offer more accurate translation of borrowed words in our language than the more formally acknowledged synonyms that fill our dictionaries—and that satisfy our vocabulary teachers, by the way. To fancy further, it is possible that slang remains truer to the spirit if not the fact of the original words than more formal modern vocabulary, for slang might have persisted throughout the centuries in popular speech with less change than the more formal language, which has sophisticated itself up through socioeconomic and educational levels away from the hard facts in which language probably had its origins. In short, the Romans might have been thinking more physically of *kicking it off* than we do of *expediting,* of *cutting the man* than we do of *homicide.*

But I do not want to follow the traditional scholar's routine toward testing my little linguistic hypothesis, and that hypothesis is not my reason for this report on my personal Latin lore. If I took the route through linguistic research, I would probably find rather early that someone else has already covered the ground, thus removing all possible joy of discovery from the territory. Therefore, I forego the famous studies of American and British slang, interesting and tempting as they may be. I am too much afraid that I will find that someone has been there before me and proven my hypothesis either right or as windy as my adolescent daydreams. And, of course, I would also thereby discover that my little linguistic hypothesis is not really mine alone after all. Furthermore, I do not want to make a career or even a formal study out of my amateur etymology, for such pursuit might destroy the whimsy, the fancy, the freedom, the fun that remain available to me without such study.

The hypothesis I do intend to raise and explore from this excursion into amateur etymology has something to do with the "difference between school and the real world," as so many of my own students have put it over the last decade and a half that I have tried to function as teacher in classes of my own. Even though it is not by any measure a huge part of my life, my peculiar brand of amateur etymology, or whatever you want to label the habit that I have been telling you about, has been for me a rich lode of interest, even entertainment. It has both amused and instructed me, in spare moments and in the rush of life at the full. Yet, beyond the general practice and method of derivation in certain vocabulary lessons—and then merely by having us "look up words in the dictionary"—my amateur etymology has had no place in formal school programs as various instructors have conceived and carried out those programs over the years that I have been a student. I am not complaining that those programs have failed to "meet the individual and his needs where he is." While individualization of instruction is my main goal as a teacher, I am experienced enough to know that given the present state of technology and school structure, extensive individualization of program remains a laudable ideal rather than a highly practicable alternative, although I shall try to offer one such alternative later in this book.

No, beyond the traditional school's failure to treat individuals as individuals, certainly the most traditional of teachers would not concede that this story of my amateur etymology deserves even a syllable in any such discussion of education as this book means to become. In their extreme, they would see no connection between what I am talking about and what they are perpetrating as an unassailable institution firmly sunk in unquestioned tradition: school. They would turn down my amateur etymology because it smacks too much of fancy or because it seems frivolous or "impractical." (I have never been able to figure out the exhaustive distinction that is apparently supposed to exist between what is practical and what is impractical in life—and thus in schooling.) Some, as I have indicated, would not allow the obvious fact of slang a place in the classroom. And, the point that the juxtaposition of the "slanginess" of adolescents with the somber formality of classical Latin is a perfect setup for humor and laughter—well, what blasphemer dare bring belly laugh into the classroom and sanctify it there? Furthermore, the creativity of the student—in this example, mine, but at any given time we are legion—too often challenges the authority or the lesson plan or the sense of direction or the mindset of the traditional instructor. Teaching-learning in the traditional setting then becomes competition, sometimes hot, usually subdued, but always prevalent, between teacher and student. Teacher always wins, at least in the immediacy of the traditional classroom (although my scholastic etymology thrives on sub rosa, for instance, whether "they" recognize it or not.)

Finally, my hypothesis questions generally the relationship between "school" and "life." Is school an accurate reflection of the life "out there," or is it not? If it is, why do so many people, especially so many students, seem to think that school is somehow different from or alienated from the mainstream of experience in the world? If school does not lead to heightened awareness of the world "out there" or if school does not effectively and efficiently prepare students for participation in life beyond school, why doesn't it? If school must continue as the institution it now is, how can the differences between supposed artificiality and apparent reality be justified? Or, if schooling is to change, how can the differences be resolved? In short, how much artificiality is there to "school," how can we determine its presence, and what can we do to replace it with genuineness and reality?

This bias of mine—and I admit that it is a bias—to see artificiality in the schools and to throw it out into the open for all to consider developed in part, as I have implied, during my own teen years. At that stage of my life, "school people" identified me at best as an individualist, at worst and more generally as a hell-raising rebel who would eventually either "grow up" and thus "grow out of such foolishness" or be silenced by the overwhelming tide of the establishment. I have yet to "grow up" in their terms, and rather than my own silencing I have found that quite legitimate critics and practitioners vocalize about the same general theme that I have been sustaining. They vocalize loud and clear and draw emphatic response from young and old, professional and lay-man alike. Furthermore, first as a teacher and then, in due process of natural drives, social customs, and love, as a parent, I have come to suspect or observe all sizes and shapes of artificiality in ele-mentary education—even in the very earliest preschool experiences of the child—from the attitudes of parents who are in some cases products of unreality in their own schooling. On another plane, as a graduate student, I have seen people victimized by similar mea-sures of artificiality on the highest levels of formal education. Some fight back.

Specifically, what's your gripe, I have been asked.

I quake at the false intonation, pace, and tone of the stereo-typed "kindergarten talk" used on the typical "tiny tots" television show and in many elementary public school classrooms. How kids can stand, in fact, how they can decipher such language, loaded as it is with phony stresses and pitches, is beyond me. The fraudu-lent language of many popular primers in elementary reading classrooms needs no further demonstration here by me. One of my colleagues, as this text is being written, is preparing a slide show in which he alternates passages from a typical illustrated primer ("This is our neighborhood. See the trees. See the wide lawns. See the daddy driving home from work.") with photographs of the slums in which millions of our schoolchildren live and where daddies either do not exist or rarely can find anyone who will hire them. I resent and am horrified by a first grade teacher's announce-ment during a PTA classroom visitation that "I tell them as long as they are quiet and busy, everything will be all right." How dare she so blatantly admit to encouraging busy work and the mere passage of time for children better suited by age and temperament to be climbing hills and running streets and digging tunnels! I shudder at long lines of six- and seven-year-olds being held outside the school building every morning and after each recess until they quiet themselves into group submissiveness so they can be permitted to enter. Nature has produced no two people so much alike and so simplistic that their self-integrity and singularity as individuals should be so denied in the name of order and monolithic authority. I suppose I might less grudgingly accept the herd-conditioning in our schools if it were not perpetrated by the same institution that claims to be helping individuals to recognize and develop their own individuality.

As a high school student and later as a teacher of English, I quailed at learning and teaching elements of a Latin grammar that was forced in the eighteenth century onto the structure of a living Germanic language, a "grammar" that has been violated regularly and successfully by the best writers and speakers of contemporary English—by Ernest Hemingway, for instance (the same man praised by teacher once we laid aside grammar handbooks and picked up literature anthologies), and by Winston Churchill and John F. Kennedy. Of course, we are to admire and believe what teacher tells us, not what we hear from men acclaimed by the world. It is a commonplace joke among high school graduates that almost all have had at least one year's exposure to American history but that hardly any have crept in that course closer to our own day and age than, say, the Spanish-American war. Cancer, heart disease, and accidents cut down more Americans each year than any other three causes of death, but high school health courses are spiked with information on yellow fever, leprosy, and the tsetse fly. Student council elections are exercises in democracy—with candidates restricted to those of the electorate who meet certain standards acceptable to school authorities, such as, B or C average, normal dresser, few or no disciplinary infractions, etc. The state licenses a sixteen-year-old to drive a $5,000 automobile down a multimillion-dollar highway, but the principal demands that he have written permission to go to the boys' room. And ghetto youths are expected to believe that America is the land of opportunity.

Colleges encourage personal responsibility through freedom of choice by compulsory attendance at lectures and by highly restrictive dormitory codes. Campus police spend more time spotting and disciplining parking violations than advisors do in helping students to plan individual courses of study. Universities honor research grants gathered by their faculties more than they honor ability and willingness to work with students. Graduate schools nurture dignity and self-awareness by ponderous mass procedures of registration that crowd thousands of students—young adults and veteran professionals—into steamy gyms where they wait in bunches for hours to accomplish ten minutes' worth of paperwork and payment. Dissertations become involuting exercises in perseverance and patience over trivialities rather than substantial contributions to knowledge and ongoing adventures in service to mankind. Such methods and practices as formal lecture and oral comprehensive examination hang over, for purposes unnecessary or impossible in twentieth-century America, from medieval Europe. On every level of education, life is fragmented, pigeonholed, labelled, and lost in the name of learning.

Listing such things that bother me is a great deal like firing a broadside from a scattergun, but focus and, I believe, positive alternatives to abuse will develop in the process of inquiry and comment through which this book will move. Concern that is initiated in personal suspicions and anger might lead to discoveries that will result in public truth and in altered direction for our schools. Some would have me specify my complaints and their solutions both at once, but I cannot do that. I want this book to allow the readers and the writer together to work through questions and alternatives, and if I am wrong in any of my suspicions and biases, together we will discover along the way that I have been wrong. Some want to learn *about* what I have to say rather than learn with me, rather than enter into the process of inquiry and discovery with me. Some want me immediately to define my conclusion—to tell them where I am headed in this inquiry so that, I guess, everyone who reads will know when I have arrived. They want me to define that conclusion even before I begin to play around with examples of what it might be, of how I might work toward a conclusion—if I ever come to one. They don't want inquiry, it seems to me; they want argument. And while a good bit of what I have to say will probably sound like argument, or rest on it, it is important to me that this personal quest, or inquiry, is always in great measure the reflection of argument that goes on within me most of the time. What sounds like statement from me is more often than not a question, for I work from the belief that ultimate and encompassing answer is ultimate death—death at least to curiosity and excitement and to some reason for looking forward to tomorrow rather than merely cursing yesterday or resigning myself to today.

Rather than state my goal, define my procedures, and tell you how I have determined that I will know I have arrived, I choose to work in somewhat of an opposite direction. Labels and definitions, even when you call them goals and couch them in the terms of disciplined inquiry, too often do more harm than good in the process of recognizing and solving problems since they tend to close minds rather than open them, to frustrate alternatives, and to cut off digression. They tend to make us overrate the accomplishment of that goal as, for instance, so many of mine honest neighbors rushing off to dear old Alma Mater Homecoming each fall trying to recapture and believe in that sense of achievement, of arrival, that they apparently experienced when they stood up and somebody handed them a diploma or when they cheered good old Monk Muscle across the goal line in the final moments of the Platinum Bowl. They tend to make us believe we actually know where we are going when in fact an accidental one-inch jerk of the steering wheel might smash life and love and faith and fundamental flat against a concrete abutment with very conclusive finality, no matter how precise the road map and how well-indexed the road. If I already know, or even can visualize to any significant degree, my goal, what joy will there be in arriving, other than knowing that I have been able to follow my own directions—or someone else's?

I choose to get no more directive nor specific at this point than to suspect that the source of my anger as it will inspire this book will become evident in at least three general abusive tendencies of many schools:

>*Insularity*. Whenever the school closes its eyes to the world around it, it is guilty of insularity. Unrealistic dress codes, the middle-class orientation of ghetto schools, irrelevance in cer-

tain subject areas of study or approaches to them—such problems are typical results of the insularity of a given school or school system.

Hypocrisy. Whenever the school fails to practice what it preaches, it is guilty of hypocrisy. The inhuman demands in time, knowledge, and attitude made by many teachers of the so-called humanities, for instance, do not generate much credence in the mind of the student. Albert Schweitzer is supposed to have said that example is not the best way; it is the only way.

Fraud or *Pretense.* Whenever the school deals in sham, whenever it tries to hoodwink its clientele, it is guilty of fraud. How many teachers have you heard who regularly use such trumped-up motivation technique as "What? You don't know what a split infinitive is! Shame on you. Did you hear that, class? Imagine! He doesn't know a split infinitive! How will you ever get into college? Believe me! We're going to take care of that right now."

It is enough to complain of irrelevance and wasted motion in the schools, but when schools compound such ills by needless abuse, ills which are often the result of pressures and restrictions beyond the immediate control of the professional educators who run the schools, I find no excuse for those "professionals" who stand guilty of maintaining or forgiving or rationalizing or ignoring such abuse.

I choose to get no more directive nor specific at this point than to suggest that there are at least three goals for education, that these also happen to be three personal goals of mine, and that whatever develops in this book will do so in the context of such goals:

–within the individual, heightened awareness of life, including sanctification of humanity,

–exchange of knowledge, perception, and belief,

–development of wisdom.

All are by nature endless and developmental, so that education is at least as much process as it is substance—probably it is more process than substance. It should bring us the sense of unity that we need within ourselves to lend order and sanity to our lives as well as the diversity required to keep us ever in motion and curious. Unity to make life whole, diversity to make it worth living. If, in institutional education, outline has replaced essence, if the individual has been lost to the institution, if accomplishment has been replaced by endurance, these purposes of education have been at least partly thwarted and to a more certain measure threatened.

2

Grading—The Hammer in Hand

Before you can properly appreciate my reaction to her big scene, you have to know how I felt about Dream Girl. Of course, she will never know I felt this way about her; her real name I shall keep secret.

She was in several ways a Dream Girl: built, beautiful, sincere —if not just the slightest bit brainy and hard-working. Given the right situation—say, she a senior that year in some high school other than the one in which I was a young, single, first-year teacher—I would undoubtedly have tried to date her. As the facts were, however, I had to play the sexless, bloodless, spineless, mechanical role known as Typical Teacher and eat my heart out, as well as about half my head, every time I saw the facts as they were walking into my classroom each day and sitting down before me: built, beautiful, sincere—if not just the slightest bit brainy, and hard-working.

That is, I felt this way for the first half of the school year or so anyway. It was precisely at the end of the third marking period that I fell violently out of love with her—all because of a scene in which she starred, a scene I have witnessed scores, even hundreds of times since then, each just as incredulously as that first time, starring both boys and girls, who were built and beautiful and sincere as well as scrawny, ugly, and insincere, and with whom I may or may not have been infatuated.

It is impossible to escape the number game these days. It crops up in education like acne in adolescence, only it has been known to be literally fatal in education. Dream Girl and I were playing one version of the number game, but she apparently had not realized its nature, and I certainly had not realized that she did not realize the nature of the game until, as I have said, the end of the third marking period.

15

The specific variety of the number game we played is called Grading, and because I was quite new to teaching, I played the game extremely close to the decimal point, you might say. Not that I took Grading too seriously myself, understand; I readily acknowledged, was even somewhat perversely proud of the several flunks and near-flunks I had picked up now and again for various nonacademic reasons during my own days as a student. But Grading being Grading, and I being a fresh young teacher, I played the game by the rule book that year.

The rule book in that school said 95-100—A, 86-94—B, and so on down the line, 95-100 of what I never have been able to figure out. I think the omnipresent 100 scale has survived from that hazy golden age when Teacher was held to be master of all knowledge and capable of determining indisputably the precise percentage of a certain portion of that omniscience which his students were able to spit back at him.

Anyhow, Dream Girl turned out a 96 in my class, I believe, by the end of the first marking period. A solid "A" on her report card. (An honest grade, by the way! As honest as the game allows. I have always bent way over not to let the facts—built, beautiful, sincere, and hard-working—get in the way of playing the game called Grading.) As I recall, her grade stood at 97 nine weeks later—a second solid "A" on the magic piece of paper. Third nine weeks it totaled 94—an obvious "B," according to the rules of the game, but just as obviously not an indication of significant change in the quality of her work, which remained superior. However, it was "B" I etched on Dream Girl's report, oblivious to any negative connotations the letter might have for her since, as far as I was concerned, the same magnificent set of facts still sat gloriously before me in the front row of my classroom five days each week. And, by this time spring had blissfully drifted up to the schoolroom window, and I was madly reckoning the days to her graduation, after which moment I might dare acknowledge myself to her as a male human being as well as a teacher and might even ask her to go to a movie with me.

Until dismissal time on report card day.

"Where have I gone wrong? Where have I gone wrong?" she stormed at herself as she trod an oval path on some imaginary plank toward the brink in front of my chalkboard. "How could I have let myself slip so badly?"

"But, you're no different! You're the same good kid and excellent student you've always been," I explained for the fiftieth time. "Look, you made a 94—the top of the B's!" I added. "It's part of the game we have to play." But the mention of the "B" shuddered her into new spasms of self-incrimination and academic masochism once again.

"You didn't drop at all, really," I continued.

"Down a whole grade and didn't drop! How can you say that? How could I have let myself down like that?"

I gave up on her that afternoon.

While I have somewhat reevaluated my working relationship to the rule book since then, I have watched reenactments of those ridiculous moments dozens of times each school year.

What is it about numbers and thinking in numerical terms that causes us to lose perspective so easily? Not only through numerical grading systems do students, educators, and parents lose this perspective. Somehow we have settled on six, for instance, as the magic number of years at which a child ought to be participating in grade one, and if the child is seven and still in grade one—oh, do we worry! Don't bother to ask whether or not anything worthwhile is going on in the child's mind or in the teacher's classroom —with or without numbers. Just make sure that certain numerical factors jibe: age six, grade one. Teacher's pay? Worry not a bit over what teacher knows or how well he can help kids to learn. Pay him by the number. It's safe, impersonal, objective (although irrelevant, more often than not). Build a sliding pay scale for him: number of years in teaching plus number of academic credits on his transcripts, and arrive at the magic number, known at this point as his salary. What are some of the most commonly debated issues in public education as heard in legislative halls or seen in newspapers and magazines? Course content? Methods of instruction? Goals of humanity? Values? Human relationships in the classroom? Rarely are such matters the center of debate. More often the issues turn on numerical factors: how many hours per day in school, how many days per year, how many courses per student, how many teachers per school, how many administrators per hundred.

Let's find a solution to the dropout problem: try to keep everyone you can in school for that magic number, twelve years, whether or not everyone needs or can understand what is going on in that school—or will help himself in the attempt.

All of these numerical concerns are without question quite important issues! But they are certainly not the only issues in education, and they definitely are not the crucial ones. Manipulate all the numerical factors listed anywhere in the preceding paragraph, and you still have not necessarily improved or harmed education, whichever purpose you held. Yet the issues of education are so often popularly treated as if there were no valid statements to be made when numbers are omitted from the conversation. If only for, say, every ten numerical statements we hear concerning education, we could hear just one healthy, purely qualitative statement like, "She's a damned good teacher because my kid loves to be with her, and he's a different and more intelligent boy for the experience. Mark her priceless!"

Perhaps such a wish is too much to ask. Education is certainly not the only part of our civilization in which most of our dialogue has turned into a reading of the slide rule. We drive coast-to-coast through this fantastic country of ours and come home to report our average daily speed, miles per gallon, number of stops per day, number of states "covered," average cost of meals. Disaster strikes —whether man-made like war or natural like earthquake. We ask first, "How many dead?" Not who has died, or whether there is any difference in anybody's life because someone else has died, or whether or not that statistic from a distant battlefield or highway accident was a man who liked chocolate ice cream better after a game of tennis than after a big meal, or how easily or uneasily he smiled when you spoke to him about his children. We first keep score, especially in fatal disasters, as if taking human life were like shooting darts.

A comment typifying the arithmetic state of mind was overheard during an intermission at a matchless performance of the magnificent play *The Royal Hunt of the Sun*, a moving dramatization of profound questions about man's relationships to fellowman, to the gods, and to self. Those questions climax in the agony of Pizarro's decision over the fate of the Inca god-king who is his prisoner. A friend of mine overheard another playgoer's explanation of the drama to his wife: "See, it's the story of how only a hundred and eighty-seven Spaniards could conquer a couple million Indians." Which, of course, it certainly is. The man in the lobby had the gross sixteenth-century headline (if there had been one), with its statistics, down pat; his figures were more or less accurate. But, oh, what he had apparently missed of the basic issues—and of life, no doubt.

Never a week goes by in the classroom without my finding at least one occasion to curse all grading systems. One morning the occasion came with the failure of eleven rather intelligent students —most of them "teacher-pleasers," by the way—to utter one upsetting, even original and sincere word in class, all of them fearing that some original observation of theirs might be "wrong" from Teacher's point of view, might incur his wrath to the point that He would record a failing index for them in His grade book. They "need" good grades to "get into college." No use thinking for oneself and coming up with an honest answer, especially an untried original one! Teacher might not welcome it; he might drop one's grade because of it!

Another day the occasion came in the fact that only after a year and a half of wearing down the benign facade of another student and finally pushing him into irrational anger was I able to get him to say what he had felt all along: that he saw absolutely no value in my literature class. Truth at last! Now, we could begin working! Truth hidden and frustrated for a year and a half by his fear of numerical retribution through my grade book. He, too, sought the numerical guarantee for college acceptance.

Not too long ago, the occasion came in the reaction of a mother who conferred with me about the lack of interest and of scholastic achievement in her son. I spent a solid half hour of honest, open, and (I thought) pertinent conversation with her: the boy is not convinced that he needs help; he probably sees no reason to take his schoolwork seriously since he already has not only unlimited freedom outside of school but also a motorcycle and an automobile of his own; he has not yet accepted repeated invitations to come to me for personal conferences about his work and his attitudes as well as mine and about what we are trying to accomplish in the course. Yes, I would welcome a chance to talk privately with him if he requested such a talk; yes, I had invited him to talk with me;

yes, I constantly hoped for a response to that invitation or for a similar invitation from him; yes, I was sincerely interested in trying to help him equip himself successfully for college in a year or two; yes, I would keep in touch with her if her son were to slide further into academic doldrums. Her reaction: a phone call to my principal the next morning, complaining that I did not seem to be very much interested in Junior as a human being because I did not even have my grade book in front of me during the interview! How could I possibly know Junior and confer intelligently with her about him if I had no record of his grades in front of me as I spoke with her? Never mind that I have a reputation for accepting students first as whatever human beings they are. Never mind that I take pride in transcending grades in my concern for the students with whom I work.

I wish her reaction were not so typical of so many people today. Unfortunately, there are parents who keep the same sort of purely numerical records, and just as extensively, on their children in school as modern dairy farmers keep on their cattle. Standard scores from kindergarten through college, I.Q.s taken at various times, number of hours of study per week, number of books read (never mind which books or how well read and whether or not they were worthwhile or enjoyable), number of As, Bs, etc., and in which subjects and when—anything that can be counted so that numerical conclusions of one sort or another can be drawn. Statistics save us the bother of facing each moment of life for whatever it brings. Statistics help us to pigeonhole our little bits of existence, to set them all in order, to add and multiply, subtract and divide them until the moment of living has been lost in computations, and "truth" stands absolute and proven, as obvious as 2 plus 2.

Oh, the arrogance involved! The arrogance of teachers who think they "have" a student in the number or letter that they scratch on his report card, who think they can judge him absolutely and capture the immeasurable complexity and grandeur of his essence in a digit or two. The arrogance of those parents who judge their children to be successes or failures by the numbers that are recorded on impersonal graphs stored in cold rows of steel file cabinets in a school office. The arrogance of students who willingly default their own humanity, their sense of their own dignity and worth, in their pursuit of such an abstract and arbitrary thing as a numerical grade! I have taught students who have been unable to write competent papers for me until I have removed the idea of grading their papers altogether. With the absence of grading, they have begun to write—and write fairly well.

How is it, really, with grading? One classroom experiment I shall never forget. The professor had reproduced enough copies of a junior high school student's arithmetic paper so that each of us future teachers in his college class could see a copy simultaneously but without conferring with each other about it. There were perhaps fifteen to twenty of us in the room.

"You have just given this boy an arithmetic test," said the professor, "and here is his paper. Grade it."

We each checked the paper carefully for about ten minutes. The problems were simple enough that everyone of us was guaranteed to see every error that appeared on it. Each of us made our notations, some wrote comments, and all of us placed a numerical grade, based on the common 100-scale, at the top of our copy of the test in hand. The professor then recorded those "grades" on the chalkboard as we reported them to him aloud.

The grades ranged from 7% to 94%. Same paper, same problems, same errors, different graders.

Now, the harpies who look into education from outside and curse it for the incompetents who can sometimes be found there, will say, "See what a bunch of ninnies those future teachers are! Low standards! Lack a clear sense of direction and definition! They obviously could not even tell right from wrong!"

Not so, not so. Easily said, but simply not so. Assume a classroom set of such papers. This boy had followed the right procedures on this problem but came up with the wrong answer. That boy used the wrong procedures but somehow came up with the right answer. This fellow, wrong procedures, wrong answer. This wrong answer obviously a slip of the pencil. That number turned around—in excitement, maybe? That simple mistake on an otherwise perfect paper. This simple mistake on a paper full of simple mistakes. That horrendous error on an otherwise perfect paper. This horrendous error on a paper full of them. This girl missed by a minute, that one by a mile. This lad skipped every other problem for what reason; that lad only one problem for what reason? Then, we turn to more human considerations, personal feelings about the various people who turned in the various papers—and to their feelings about you and the school and arithmetic and the exam. Or, to the various attitudes and personal situations that the various students brought immediately to the exam when it fell before them on the desk, or to their records of achievement and attitude from the past. This boy missed every problem last week, missed only one this week. That boy worked half the problems successfully last week, half this week. This one dropped. Or, to the test itself: Every kid in class missed #8 the same way, or half missed #6 the same way, or all missed #4 different ways. And on and on.

As a system, grading leads us to believe that it is based on absolutes. We are so long into the system that we have tended to believe there is such a thing as 100 or 95 or 75 or whatever and that it has exactly the same meaning to everybody who sees it or uses it as a grade. We are victims of this marvelous gift of ours called language, the vehicle that has brought us the wisdom of the ages. And the vehicle that has made it possible for man, and man alone of all the animals, to lie.

Without language, a dog realizes that a bucket of hot water is a bucket of hot water because he gets his nose scalded when he dips it into the water expecting a touch of cool water. But, if a man is convincing enough with his words, he can warn his child not to try the water for fear of scalding. Or, if he is inclined in another direction, he can trick some fool into momentarily believing that the hot water is really not hot water until the fool, like the dog, gets his nose scalded by actual experiment.

Of course, there is further difficulty with those language habits we call our grading system. At least the words "hot water" have a physical referent by which we can measure the accuracy of the words. We can dip into the water or, better yet, stick a thermometer into it to see whether or not the H_2O in that bucket is indeed "hot water." Not so with a grade. The numbers and letters we have grown to accept as grades have been conceived and are assigned most arbitrarily. There is no physical referent behind them. Ah, yes, if we give the student ten problems in simple addition and we find that he successfully adds all ten lists of numbers, we can easily agree to give him "100" on the test.

Or can we agree to do so that easily? Can we not just as easily offer any of a number of other statements about grading the same group of ten problems:

"Now, class, this quiz is worth 15 points—one and a half points for each correct answer."

"Children, this test will determine whether or not you repeat this unit of work in simple addition. Either you solve all ten problems successfully, or you repeat the entire unit."

"Now, boys, each problem is worth 100 points. Let's see who can bat 1.000." (And notice how "one thousand" is properly printed as a figure in batting average.)

Or we could even say, "Your grade on this quiz will determine whether or not you fail for the year," and then later throw the unread papers into the waste basket and deny that we ever said anything like that.

I had a philosophy professor in my sophomore year at college who drove most of us wild by his grading system, mainly because we could figure out no normal numerical rationale behind it at all. Each examination he gave us included three essay questions that seemed equal in depth and difficulty; yet the single grade he assigned on the entire examination was invariably based on a perfect score of 40—far beyond the computation of us simplistic sophomores, oriented as we were by long years of infliction of the 100-scale.

In accumulating numbers of dollars, the miser at least has the satisfaction of knowing he can exchange his dollars anytime he chooses for beans or baubles or a bigger gunnysack. In accumulating grades, no such assurance is possible. We do not limit full servings in the school lunchroom to only those students who collect straight As leaving the flunkies to starve to death. Nor do those As guarantee success in life. Often they are achieved at the expense of the very goal of education as a heightened awareness of life, as when kids hole themselves up in closets full of homework every waking moment out of school rather than seek direct experiences with life and other people. It is almost cliché for teachers to note how many high school "goof-offs" have become some of the most successful businessmen in town and how often the girl (it's so terribly often a girl, I wonder that positions of world leadership have so long been held by men) at the top of her class turns into a run-of-the-mill housewife a few years later. Given my choice of two guides to steer me through the intricacies of everyday life in the contemporary downtown area, the bookish scholar with the straight-A average or the flunkie who has grown up in the street, I'll take the flunkie—and survival.

Grading is not based on absolutes; it is quite arbitrary. In practice, it involves an infinite number of variables, even when a class of future teachers is grading identical copies of a junior high arithmetic exercise. A hit in the "7" wedge on a dartboard is a hit in the "7" wedge, and, in one dart game at least, it counts for seven points. I have noticed on some dartboards that the various areas of the boards, with their various scoring capacities, are now trimmed with thin metal strips to bring arbitration over borderlines to naught, to prevent the dart from ending dead center on the line between two areas. But human beings and the work they produce and the tests they complete are not metal-lined dartboards; they are not so absolutely defined and scored. Nor is a teacher or a pupil or a test as simple nor as incisive nor as clinical as a dart.

I could go on for the next one hundred pages bemoaning the failure of our grading system to serve as the expedient it is meant to be at communicating one person's level of achievement or ability to someone else. It is bad enough that at best it fails to measure more than a pinch of what a person knows, and then with so many chance factors involved that we must suspect the measurement of that pinch. It is worse that it rarely or never measures how that person feels or what he believes or hopes or dreams or fears. It is tragic when some abstract and relative letter or number leads us around, a figment of our own imaginations. If we are interested in an individual's learning through a school system, we will develop a system that allows (yea, encourages) him to learn, then credits him with whatever he learns. If he does not know something today, we will hope he might know it tomorrow. The grading system too often cuts him off from that opportunity or discourages any desire within him to try again tomorrow. If someone is going to dangle a carrot in front of me to entice me to move in a certain direction, it damn well better be a carrot that can be touched and tasted once I have moved. At this point, we will not argue over direction moved and who has decided on that direction and why. We have a lengthy quest ahead of us, with room for that consideration later.

3

Certification—Rubber Stamps and Stamina

The troubles with our credentialling symbols and the system behind them are about the same as the troubles with our grading system. Outline has replaced essence, symbols have remained relatively stable from a simpler civilization, while referents have shifted and proliferated and intensified and specialized and become more complicated all over the place. If we were true to the simplistic medieval tenor of the tradition of academic degrees, for instance, we should be hard put to tell a Doctor of Feet from a Doctor of Philosophy, for both titles derive from Latin *doceo*, "I teach," and from the medieval marriage between monastic scholarship and trade guild licensing of practitioners.

Titles today do not tell us much at all about what their holders know or what they can do or how well. Ten different members of the same high school graduating class, receiving identical diplomas, can easily have undergone ten different programs with ten entirely different measures of success. A graduate student might be granted a Doctor of Philosophy degree for a highly technical, extremely nonphilosophical, statistical, or otherwise narrowly specialized project.

At the same time, we have imbued academic symbols with certain hocus-pocus for various reasons and thus further obscured any specific significance or achievements of their holders. I think it is interesting, for instance, that if a kid quits school after grade eight, we say he has had eight years of schooling. But if he perseveres four more years—through grade twelve—something magical apparently happens, for suddenly he has not simply had twelve years of schooling, he is now a high school graduate! So, hats fly and flashbulbs pop, and he can pity or sneer at the eighth-grade quitter or even at the eleven and a half-year quitter, and jobs open and he can join particular branches of the Navy. Or, just let him stick out schooling for four more years, and he has not simply had sixteen years of schooling; rather, he wins a bachelor's degree of one kind or another which works greater mystical wonder for him than the high school diploma. And on and on up the ladder—piling something, we are not sure what, higher and deeper.

Oversimplification or not, the typical doctorate today does not represent a movement in its individual holder from a narrow early education up through the years to all-encompassing breadth commensurate with the holder's chronological maturity. Rather, the magnificent panorama of life as he perceives it is his natural province, the natural arena of his curiosity, when he is preschool or elementary age, but once into high school his academic program begins to specialize, rather easily at first. Then, through the "liberal" arts and sciences of his undergraduate course in college, he specializes rather abruptly—almost always with a single "major" discipline—and by the time he gets into advanced graduate work, he has narrowed attention to "Comparison of Two Separate Manifestations of the Hyperinsulinism Syndrome in One of the Minor Characters in *Rex Ruminas Rex*, an Unpublished Novel by Thesus Thespian, Court Jester to His Eminence Frederick the Flat."

Unfortunate but popular misconceptions accrue about the various symbols and steps in this whole process. Some folks think that the various symbols represent learning—either its extent or size or depth or breadth or whatever. And some folks equate learning with sense, or sense with schooling, or schooling with learning—but all of this kind of simplistic equation is up for question.

I love the story of the physics professor—good man, good teacher—who quite capably instructed his classes on water pressure and confluence and screw principle and gravity. But, the day a water pipe burst in his laboratory and leaked gallons of water into the library one floor down, he had no idea where or how to turn the proper valve to save the books from a bath.

Or, of the employer who thought he had at last devised a simple but foolproof means of certification by which to determine the qualifications of applicants for a position as clerical assistant in his office. His version of the "comprehensive qualifying examination":

"If a customer overpays his bill by ten dollars, what would you do with the extra ten?"

The first girl decides that she would return ten dollars to the customer, the second that she would remit a credit slip for ten dollars, the third that she would throw the ten dollars into petty cash and forget about it. Which girl, then, does he hire? Naturally, the one with the best-looking miniskirt.

In a way, we spend a great deal of time and effort and sincerity and folklore trying to uphold a system of academic credentialling and job certification that looks like stable, objective, sensible measurement and communication of pertinent variables, but in the crucial moment of decision it is, after all, so often the miniskirts of the moment that make up our minds for us.

Or, the notion grows that a person must hold a certain symbol of education before he can perform some task or serve in some capacity that may or may not have any direct relationship with the education he has undergone. My service station man has owned and operated a successful gas station along a busy main highway for twenty years or so, but he was prevented from applying for the more lucrative management of a nearby turnpike gas station for the same oil company because he held no college degree. By similar nonlogic, many positions in our schools may not be serviced legally by highly qualified professionals simply because that medical doctor or artist or cabinetmaker or stenographer or news reporter or fish and game warden or research chemist has not picked up fifteen or eighteen or twenty-four "hours" of education coursework somewhere along the way.

Some of us, you see, can use this academic symbology, however empty or erring it may be overall, to make life easier for ourselves —to save us the bother or embarrassment or effort of human-to-human confrontation and recognition in depth or reality. Three times as many applicants for managing turnpike gas stations than there are positions to be filled? Easy—cut two-thirds of the applicants by requiring a college degree that most of them probably will not have. Want an inexpensive ritual to bring some semblance of unity and finish to the twelve years of conglomerate the seventeen-year-old has just survived? Top off those years with a cap and a gown and a handshake over the sheepskin. Need a mask for the fact that numbers and letters and grades of all kinds and duration and endurance all have replaced essence and experience and

achievement in our educational system? Build sentiment and tradition and job security and status into symbols that have lost their
original meanings.

As a young teacher, I was working hard each summer in an
expensive, demanding, somewhat selective, magnificently staffed,
quality graduate program of studies toward a master's degree. At
about the same time, a fellow teacher was picking up much faster,
much easier credits toward a master's degree from a nearby degree
mill—one that churned them out by the thousands, a dollar down
and degree in a year.

"So why are you working so hard, Kline? When we're done,
we'll both be at the same point on the salary scale—a master's
degree. In fact, I'll get there faster than you. Who out there knows
the difference?"

"You're right," I admitted, "but you and I will know the difference." And we do, but the difference is not apparent in the
degrees we hold. I tell the story simply to illustrate the way that
our certification habits and symbology so easily turn upside down
on us.

A high school senior, respected president of his class and excellent student, pointed to similar loss of meaning in academic symbology when he suggested that graduation exercises be dropped
since "Graduation doesn't mean anything anymore—not what it
might have at one time. Today, everybody passes, sooner or later
—we know that—and everybody graduates—everybody, as long as
he behaves himself and gets the right teachers and puts up with
enough or waits long enough." Similarly, it is now rather common,
especially at large universities where they can hardly be missed, for
students to skip their own commencement exercises.

Schools, in turn, have attempted to rectify matters, not by
questioning the traditional methods of certification and whether
or not they can any longer perform the task of communication
and licensing that the process was originally designed to perform,
but by trying to preserve the system, by proliferating symbols, for
instance, so that some of them might more nearly describe what a
person knows or can do or has achieved. There are now, for instance, over three thousand different academic degrees that can be
earned in various school programs in the United States.

There is no question about it: our certification procedures have
outlived the effectiveness for which they were designed; the effects

of status they now wield are fallacious and distorting in reflecting their holders' capabilities as individuals; and a good bit of the fault lies in our failure to adjust those certification practices, that institution within education, to meet the needs of a society and of schooling that were undreamed of when present frameworks for certification were formulated centuries ago. A different kind of population is now being served by our schools, one that includes everyone, not just the clerics and a few scholars. Those schools are expected to provide education in just about everything—comprehensive education, it is called. But the mechanism by which an individual's qualification as an educated person is "represented" remains patterned on that high church, exclusive church, semi-secret, simplistic, medieval European model of monastic training aimed at disseminating narrowly orthodox, globally single-celled wonders of Augustinian or early Franciscan Christianity. As Western civilization has democratized and exploded into incredible multiplicity and as schools in the last century and a half have attempted to meet the new age—especially in bustling nineteenth-century America, with its very shallow tradition of scholarship and intellectuality for its own sake—the massive surge of the upwardly mobile population has found most of us adopting the headier elements, the trappings and framework of the European tradition (for respectability) while demanding the pragmatic usefulness and functionalism that once kept the farm going and that now are needed for business and industry. We want a monk's hood that doubles as mallet to beat the rhythms of the workaday world, an ivory tower that serves also as windmill to grind the daily grains of commerce.

Little wonder that we are in the dilemma we are in when we look for specific substance behind the symbols we so glibly accept as sacred. Little wonder that many of us view the process in general as a simple matter of institutional rubber stamping for anyone who has stamina to outlast the system—or to outwit it. For there is no question that the system can be outsmarted or subverted. There are so many different ways to pick up a diploma or a degree that I sometimes wonder why any of us bother with any of it—cheaply, expensively, sincerely, or cynically.

Defenders of the general certification process cite safety as one reason for maintaining the institution. Certification, credentialling, requirements are the net needed to snare any cads who might try to bound undeservingly through the system and into respectability at the other end. I myself certainly feel more comfortable thinking that the nurse drawing blood from my arm has been trained in blood-drawing and not in plumbing, but that does not prevent her from being, in fact, an inept nurse. Furthermore, my suspicion is that the bounders get through as it is and that the system defended as safeguard probably does as much damage as good. For instance, I never fail to be disturbed that the academic establishment so often has placed itself in the embarrassing position of being last to certify (or perhaps attract into certification procedures) some of humanity's most creative individuals—Mark Twain, Einstein, Churchill, Frost, to name four famous ones. How many lesser personages, also quite creative or intellectual or valuable but simply not famous, have gone equally unrecognized in their early lives and unattracted by formal educational institutions? On the other end of humanity's scale of personal abilities, why must education's habit of certification so brutally punish those who do not measure up to some institutional yardstick that someone somehow somewhere apparently decided was "norm"? If we are to talk of individualized learning, we are to talk of individualized learning, and that means we worry first about individuals and their learning. Yet, by our belief that we need some sort of identifying stamp of institutional approval, we turn ourselves into hypocritical brutes rather abruptly, and all through a custom that glistens with polished respectability and no small dash of pomp—diplomas, degrees.

I have centered in, here, on diplomas and degrees rather heavily, but the abuse of misapplied or distorted certification is all around us in education. It is evident in gold stars, blue stars, and bunny stickers, in red pencils that mark "wrongs" rather than draw attention to rights. It is painfully evident everytime someone pretends there can honestly be such a thing as an oral *comprehensive examination*—a valid exercise in determining the extent of what someone knows or how he thinks. The inherent presumption! It shows up in our popular views of final exams and midyear exams—that they somehow measure a person's learning or serve as the payoff of his education or determine whether he is or is not "worth the institution's further effort." I am as baffled now as I was the first time I heard of them about what is the significance for learning in "semester hours" and "credit hours" and "quality points" and "cumulative averages" and "Carnegie units." I will never forget standing in the rest room after my college commencement exercises, certificate of bachelor of arts in one hand, wondering what it meant by itself and why the world seemed to insist so hard that it be given me only after one hundred and twenty hours of "work" (plus four, if I remember well, in "physical education" and a certain number of chapel services attended). We *promote* a child and parents rejoice; we *flunk* him and—it happens, you know —suicide ensues. When will educational institution accept a person for what he is? When will it quit getting in the way of the basic human relationships that mankind so much needs? When will it stop playing terrible games?

It was the last class before Christmas vacation, and the math professor slipped us a nine-question quiz. Now, I was not entirely surprised when I presented my paper to him and stood by completely befuddled as my stupidity in his version of freshman mathematics ruined his little vacation treat for us—honestly, in his mind, a clever little device to extend season's greetings.

The catalog had advertised his course as "mathematics for those who think they will never need mathematics again," and, brother, I was one of those! So, I signed up. My first lesson in realizing that catalog descriptions might better be written by students than by professors. Of twenty-eight starters, seven of us "who will never need mathematics again" eventually passed the course. I was not among the seven.

Thus, no surprise when he checked my answers quickly on the nine-point Christmas quiz, muttered a *sorry*, then a *hmmm*, a *huh*, two or three shrugs, and a final "Oh, well. . . ."

But up until the "Oh, well" he really had me confused, for after the third question (which I had solved correctly) he had written an "R," after the sixth, an "X," and after the ninth, an "S." "R" for "Right"? "X" for "Wrong"? "S" for what in the world?

"Oh, well," he smiled, "Merry Christmas anyhow, Kline." And, he filled in the letters he must have expected to fill in beside nine correct answers to a "snap" quiz on everyone's paper: M-E-R-R-Y-X-M-A-S.

Thank goodness, friendship survived between us, a fact reinforced a year later when I happened to meet him in pleasant conversation hundreds of miles away where he was in a new job that he had taken at the end of my freshman year—whether or not because of me and my kind, I have never tried to determine. But at the moment of the R-X-S incident, we were hardly friends. From my guilt and frustration and anger and inferiority, I hated him! And mathematics loomed more than ever before a misery that stood in my way between sufficient semester hours and proper grade quotient to keep me in college and my potential as a learner in search of a heightened awareness of life and the development of wisdom.

My quarrel is not with the people in education, generally, unless or until they insist, sometimes blindly, sometimes blithely, sometimes brutally, on defending one or more components of a system that no longer serves their own stated purposes: facilitated learning for every individual, based on *his* needs and *his* immediate abilities. Rather, my hope is that we might devise a system that will more readily allow such goals to be realized than any that I now see in operation.

Nor can I pretend that my own academic degrees mean nothing to me or that I myself have not looked to high standards and quality performance and challenge as laudable elements of an educational program. I merely recognize that standards and quality and challenge are highly relative concepts once they are applied to activities in our schools, say, and that my degrees might mean little or nothing to anyone else, and that they certainly do not tell anyone very specifically who or what I am or what I know or can do or feel or believe and how deeply or well or extensively. Conversely, I recognize that my degrees and diplomas and grade records might signify far more to certain other people than they should—that many of us are indeed caught up in the hocus-pocus and romantic glorification and pseudo-mysticism and easy labelling of academic symbology. And I am keenly aware of the market values such symbols accrue in a society obsessed with such pseudo-mysticism.

I fully recognize, then, that whatever realistic meaning various academic "certificates" or "credentials" now have, the meaning resides mostly with the individual holder of the individual diploma or degree or license or whatever. That symbol is private in meaning, of course, as the meaning of all symbol, of all language is at last private to the individual who develops and uses it. But it is private in meaning, too, in that only the holder knows what the diploma or degree or certificate represents in effort, in achievement, in learning, in experience, in quality, and the rest. The certificate *does not communicate well* at all.

As we shape an alternative to our present system of education, or as we at least dream one, let us fashion a system that strengthens personal meaning or significance for its individual participants—for each of them in his own sacred, private way. Then, let us try to develop a system of reporting that more accurately communicates whatever that individual thinks someone else ought to know about him and his learning or achievement or experience or quality and the rest. Perhaps we will yet build an educational system that can accept an individual for whatever he is—as contributor or as receiver or as observer. Perhaps we will yet welcome whatever he can contribute to society at large and, in education, to the institution itself and credit him for the offer.

4

What We're Up To and Why

I remember hearing Robert Frost berate a group made up mostly of English teachers one summer evening in the late fifties at the Bread Loaf School of English in Vermont. "The trouble with most of you teachers," he said (or words to this effect), "is that you never climb out on top of the pile of all that stuff you're teaching and doing—you never climb out on top once in awhile and ask *why*."

I suppose I recall that charge so vividly not only because it came from the unforgettable presence of one of the most imposing personalities of our century, but probably more because I had been taking moments to do just what Frost was saying we teachers did not do often enough—I had been climbing out on top of the pile once in awhile and asking why. I had been taking such moments as a young teacher for two or three years, just as I had taken them many, many times for what seemed then like years and years as a still younger student. For instance, I knew exactly why I had "taught" Shakespeare's *Julius Caesar* to Josh Jones and his infamous 9E group (rock bottom gang), most of whom could not read at all above a second-grade level. Oh, I made up lots of excuses and hopes for doing *Caesar* with them—historical background, literary appreciation, human understanding, universality, last chance to cram "culture" into those imminent dropouts, etc., etc. But, the major reasons why I taught them *Caesar* were that I did not know what else to do with them, and all I had that we could make a "class" out of (besides people) was twenty-five copies of an old anthology that had *Caesar* in it, among other things.

That is pretty much why I taught the eight parts of speech that year as well as the four structural kinds of sentences (simple, compound, complex, compound-complex) and the four types of sentence by purpose or tone (declarative, interrogative, imperative, exclamatory). Although there were other reasons why some of these latter items entered into my ninth-grade English course: (1) the kids had not "learned it" in eighth grade or in seventh grade or in sixth or in however many other lower grades the same basic material had been presented to them; (2) they were going to move on (don't force me to tell you why or how they were going to do that) to another teacher who would, when she discovered their appalling ignorance about such matters literary and grammatical, blame me for not having taught them well; (3) then, too, there were very real limitations of personal time and energy and ability. Just how does one underweight, nervous neophyte begin meeting the educational needs of 175 adolescents in a course called English? What is needed and what is not? Important and not? For which individuals of the 175? With what timing and frequency and duration for each? To what ends and with what varying degrees and kinds of motivation and ability and interest, or lack of such? How to do all this once you center on what you think might be answers to all these questions? Sooner or later—even without the book-keeping and housekeeping of selling tickets, collecting permission slips, taking attendance, ordering supplies, checking halls, policing cafeterias, and on and on—even without all that, one comes to ask how he might survive the day, not accomplish anything in it, but simply survive it. Easy enough: one drills on eight parts of speech, tests on them, and records As for the kids who would have had As before the drill and Fs for the kids who have succeeded only in hating the experience a bit more than they did last year—or in becoming harder to it.

At the end of that first year of teaching, I saw little accomplishment but felt crushing frustration. It was then that I announced to my department chairman, a lady rather responsible for drawing me into teaching English in the first place, that teaching was not for me, and I told her the main reason why it was not for me: Never had I spent more effort with greater ideal and come up with so meager a result—little more than personal survival. It was then that she confided what she considered the achievement of her first year as a teacher: "I was pleased by June that when I asked my students to sit down, they sat down." Such a comment from such a teacher—she is among the finest by anyone's standards and was so then—kept me in the classroom for the next year and the next, and now I don't want to get out.

Still, it is too often true that one survives the day, the week, the year, the school by lowering expectations or by compromising belief or by swallowing conviction and certainly by immersing oneself in the pile so as to anesthetize against asking, "Why am I up to what I am up to?" Perhaps it is such frustration that led to the coining of that old adage in the teaching profession: "If you have taught one person one thing in one year, your year has been successful." Or, from an administrator's point of view, as related to me by an assistant principal with whom I worked, "If you get through to June and haven't been assaulted, sued, or fired, your year has been a success."

One day, just a few months ago, a student teacher came to me with her first problem. She had been observing traditional sophomore or junior English classes with an experienced high school teacher in charge and now was to pick up one section and become its "teacher."

"I meet my first class—Mrs. Pieper's class—next Monday, and I want some ideas on how to make it interesting to the kids."

"What's the topic?" I asked.

"Walt Whitman's life," she replied.

In one day? The whole life? To what end? Why? How? Who cares? Why Walt Whitman? Anything about his poetry? Why that? All his poetry? To what end? How to read it? Why bother reading it? As it might reflect one man's view of life? As Americans? As nineteenth-century American culture? As a poet? As a person? What are we up to?

"Because Mrs. Pieper told me to teach Walt Whitman's life that day."

"Did she tell you why? Did she offer a context for the lesson?"

"It's an American Lit course."

"For all juniors? What kinds of juniors? American literature chronologically, by theme, by type? Why?"

"I guess. She didn't say. Yes. . . . Oh, you know, it's always been taught that way! I can't help it. She decided what the lesson was going to be about. Don't ask me."

Most of us as individual educators do not really know why we teach what we are teaching the way we are trying to teach it. We rarely build a rationale from naked ground up. Usually, we teach what we were taught as we were taught it, or we simply take the textbook from the shelf and move from page one through June.

Or we accept outline without essence, as, for instance, most applicants for teaching positions can specify whether they want to teach "tenth-grade English" or "eleventh-grade English." As a department chairman responsible for interviewing applicants, I was always nonplussed at anyone's ability to determine with some apparent certainty that he could teach tenth-grade English but not twelfth, or twelfth but not ninth. How could one be so sure before he was able to identify some significant difference between the content of tenth-grade English and that of twelfth-grade English? Personally, I have taught "English" formally on every grade level from eighth through college sophomore and was able to define little or no difference in what I was basically trying to be about. What is there in tenth-grade English that is not in twelfth? Titles might differ and people certainly differ, but are there two different kinds of English—one for fifteen-year-olds and a distinct one for seventeen-year-olds? We are so long into the outline, into the game of boxes and grade levels and courses and classifications by date and by number that we think that outline describes essential differences in content and sophistication, which it might but which it more often does not do.

Shall I ever forget Ron Hardin, two-time loser in my sophomore English class that traumatically instructive first year of my career? Ron had already passed English III and was passing English IV, but he was spending his third year in English II. Why? Lack of knowledge? Inability to meet some sort of curricular goals unique to English II? Hardly. He gleefully offered to peddle answers to every question I asked in class about the subject matter at hand. He and I knew—and you can surmise—why he was spending his third year in English II. He and the former teacher simply hated each other! Little wonder that he called me his "savior."

Exactly what are we up to in this thing called curriculum and instruction in our courses and credits and coverage and continuity? What have you really learned by the end of the course? Who decides? By what criteria? To what effect? I can tell you partly why I became an English teacher. It had little to do with curriculum, for I thought most of the "grammar" lessons were foolish and fallacious, I rarely read literary assignments the whole way through (if I read them at all), and the "assigned" writing that I did more often than not was an attempt at self-explanation and therapy (!)

rather than at meeting curricular specifications. (I think I must have become the only college freshman in the world granted special permission by the instructor to enroll in an Advanced Exposition class without knowing what anyone meant by "exposition" —how it differed from any other kind of writing.) No, my becoming an English teacher rather than some other kind of teacher resulted in no small measure from the fact that my senior English teacher in high school was the one person in the world— or at least in the educational world—who took time, who made me believe she even wanted, to sit down and listen to the rantings and tribulations and dreams and wild ideas of a confused, excited, scared, thunderstruck boy in the late forties.

Why did I almost leave English and switch to geology two years later? Because of a course of study? Because of a sudden switch to scientific bias? Because of some inevitable revelation of geological truth reflected in a formal curriculum? No, more because of admiration for several of the geology instructors—one a zealous, fiery, intelligent, driving, articulate, courageous lame man who on crutches led us healthy young bulls over rugged mountainsides and shifting acres of shale and muck and bramble of riverbed, who led us at a pace and with a sureness that left us always yards and minutes behind him, panting and aching and open-eyed.

What are we up to and why in this thing called teaching and learning? My second grader comes home and talks about "our Alaska unit"—polar bears and blubber, Eskimos and igloos—and I wonder what, how, and why. Why Alaska? Why not Bali? Why not Timbuktu? Why not Utopia—and whose? I am reminded of the only item I remember from my own fourth-grade curriculum —or was it third, or sixth? My Egypt poster. I wonder what the course of study said we were learning with that project or what the teacher announced she was teaching. Each kid was assigned a different country and was to produce a single poster about it. I remember carefully cutting and trimming pictures from *National Geographic* and thinking how unfortunate it was that in cutting a picture from one page, I had to decimate a picture or two on the other side of that leaf. Then, the careful arrangement of pictures on poster board—proportion and color and shape and border—with extra caution for dirty fingers and the trickiness of glue that so easily spread too far and caused a smudge. And the tremulous journey to school, shielding the huge heavy paper from wind and tree and schoolmate. And the warnings and advice from older sisters and neighborhood kids who had taken the same kinds of posters to the same teacher under similar circumstances in previous years. And, finally, there it was on a bulletin board—tacked among Iceland and Australia and Japan. And, that's what I learned about geography, I guess—or was it social studies? Ah, no! How can I ever forget? It was Egypt—whatever that was.

What are we up to and why? After I had been a teacher for most of a decade or so, we formed a language arts curriculum committee to study our curriculum from kindergarten through grade 13—grade 13 to symbolize the open-endedness of it all. I wondered what it was necessary for a third grader, for instance, to know about his language, and I hoped we might ruminate about that question a bit. But an older and wiser committee member simply reached for the current third-grade language arts textbook and read from the table of contents, and when my objection became too insistent, someone pulled me aside and said quietly and benevolently, "Yes, yes, it's nice to ask these questions of yours: what is it necessary to know, and when, and for which kids, and all that. But, you see, we have this huge inventory of materials, this huge investment in textbooks on the shelves, and we cannot, after all, expect to throw them out, and . . . ." How many needed changes have gone unidentified, how many questions never asked, how many abuses continued in our schools, how many "courses of study" turned into tables of immutable marble simply because someone has developed some rationalization to excuse and protect some weighty investment intruding massively from the past?

Don't ask such basic questions, I am advised. Don't start from nothing and build from there. You will succeed only in reinventing the wheel. Ah, yes, say I. Then, let me reinvent the wheel. At least I will have learned in the process why I have invented it and what it is all about and how I have invented it and what good it is. At least I will have learned all that. And maybe, just maybe, I will not reinvent the wheel at all. Maybe I will come up with the air cushion, as Detroit has done too late, and save the billions and billions of dollars' worth of civilization that is tied, now, to the wheel and its insatiable demand for ever more expensive highways.

So I bother with such questions—turn them over all the time. Why teach anything that we teach? Why history, science, math, and language? What is so sacred about that big four? Why not Change and Love and Continuity and Cows? You might build up a good rationale for them, and in time, with enough investment in time and materials and human belief, my C_3L curriculum—sensible or not—might be granted the same kind of sanctity now accorded the traditional, unchallenged, hand-me-down curriculum. Nothing has bothered me so much as those attempts at so-called "curriculum reform" which have begun not with the question, "What is it necessary to know?" but rather with, "How can we better teach what we have been up to?" I do not want a reform committee to study the mathematics curriculum or the one in science or social studies or Hemstitching I. I want a curriculum committee to study life, to begin from there and try to determine what schools should be up to in relation to life. Too many attempts at "curriculum reform" have not been that at all; rather, they have been systematic attempts to develop new ways to teach the old things—how to make them interesting or relevant or effective or efficient or "fun" or how to let the student "discover" rather than "be told." I love the so-called discovery method of inductive teaching, but I love it mainly because I so much distrust what it is supposed to replace— the more traditional "3-R" approach to teaching: Receive, Repeat, Reward. "Discovery" method as now being introduced in many schools reminds me of Hansel and Gretel picking their way out of the woods by following the bread crumbs—crumbs they have dropped, yes, but along the wicked old stepmother's or the miserable father's path, after all. Will we ever reach the point of allowing them to develop paths of their own, if they want to try —discovery as the first man discovered from listening to his own blood run, his own breathing and from embarking from there on the history of man, on humanity's adventure of spirit into matter, to borrow a favorite phrase from some of Robert Frost's "conversations" in Vermont.

That is not to say there should be no course of study—not at all. If a well-defined course of study is not absolutely always necessary, it is at least desirable. It makes it easier for the teacher, and hopefully for the student as well, to retain a feeling of sanity, if sanity can be defined as a "momentary stay against confusion," to borrow one of Frost's definitions of poetry. I simply wish that we might seek the basic structures of knowledge—yea, of life—that Jerome Bruner pushes us toward in *The Process of Education*— those universal truths or at least beliefs or perhaps processes or whatever that can be recognized by anyone at any age if he meets them in a language he can understand and on his own level of sophistication. I simply wish we might take literally the suggestion of Dwight Allen: that in shaping a new education, we might begin by saying, "Here is what the ideal education would be, the best we can dream up." Then, in seeking support and implementation, we would say, "And here are our available resources. They allow us to develop this much of our ideal educational program." Instead, we continue to carpenter spare 2 $\times$ 4s onto a pile of ramshackle antique in the name of curriculum reform.

Of course, I am fully aware of the difficulties involved in the sort of question I propose and of the incredible magnitude of the project. I am aware of many of the attempts to spell out a course of study, to set it down on paper. The extreme liberals and romantics and idealists among us come out with the marvelous chestnut about "Mark Hopkins on one end of a log with a student at the other." Great! The whole course of study—Kindergarten through Infinity—in one fine chestnut shell. The liberal-romantic-idealist within me throbs to have it in the classroom. Alas, however, in most classrooms there is not a log to be had. And how often, these days, do you run into a teacher named Mark Hopkins? Instead, in some of the more daring schools, thanks to the computers et al., you find mods and pods, and in every school, daring or not, the familiar mixture of gods and clods that has been with mankind since that first thunderous clap of school bell in the great long ago. And all of them—mods, gods, pods, clods—seem to grow more numerous each September, while Mark's log has turned pretty much into a toothpick factory.

At the other extreme sit the conservatives and pragmatists and realists. They reach for the best-selling textbooks and anthologies, workbooks and study guides, open to the various tables of contents, and write a thoroughly teachable, testable (and too often detestable) course of study. Finally! The disciplinarian within me marches into classroom well-armed and clear of mind and eye. Then, sooner or later, world and classroom merge, and (in English, for instance) I realize how tangled I have become in a repetitious, inhuman list composed exclusively of such items as Parts of Speech or Phonemes and Morphemes; "I" before "E"; the Comma, Colon, Carat, Dash; Kinds of Sentences or Kernel Sentences: Declarative, Imperative, Interrogatory, Exclamatory or Simple, Compound, Complex, or N-V, N-V-N, N-V-N-N. The course of study in Literature reads strictly by Title or Type, occasionally by Theme or Time: *Julius Caesar* (9), *The Merchant of Venice* (10); American Lit (11), *Macbeth* (12). (Memo to Eng. Dept.: Spot any inconsistency you can.) Let a student ask for "relevance," and we replace the universally mandated *Macbeth* with the universally mandated *A Separate Peace*.

What to teach and why? How to find connection between whale oil and Woodrow Wilson? Maybe the result of incipient senility in impending middle age, a very crazy thought crossed my mind—and stuck halfway across—one day not too long ago. In trying to draw up an innovative curriculum to suggest during an inservice workshop for teachers, one of us simply remarked that the kids whom these teachers are now teaching will probably live most of their lives in the twenty-first century. And there sat I, with my 1931 birthright, pretending to be able to advise teachers what it will be necessary for their kids to know in the year 2019. So, I subtracted a hundred years across the board and wondered what advice my Vintage 1831 predecessor might have offered to the fledglings of his day.

"Remember, your students will be living in the year 1919," he might have said. "The way things are going right now, the whole world should be on whale oil by then!" As whale oil went, so will go Xerox and IBM and Cape Kennedy, maybe? It is so impossible to guess at the Versailles of 1919 when the smoke is still clearing from Gettysburg in the sixties. So I settle for asking, "What knowledge or belief or process or whatever did man in 1830 hold in common with man in 1919?" And maybe it is also fruitful to ask, from the vantage point of 1970, "What could the 1831 man have suggested to the 1870 students to prepare them for the world of 1919?" I doubt if we will agree on any absolute answers. We might not even arrive at any answers—most likely nothing but more questions. But maybe, just maybe, we will discover some meaningful relationship between whale oil and Woodrow Wilson.

And, if we do, we might call it education and publish the glad tidings abroad and live happily ever after.[1] If we do not discover such resolution, I am sure we will at least have developed for ourselves a strong and demanding educational perspective on what we are up to and why.

For openers, I would like to acknowledge at least six different kinds of curricula available to us. Whether or not any of them allows us to define an immediate relationship between whale oil and the eminent President of the United States during World War I, I would not swear. But I am willing to say that taken as a group, they are comprehensive of mankind's capabilities and that as separate categories, they can be rather clearly distinguished from each other. Goals and procedures from each kind are now at work in our schools, whether or not we recognize the parameters and distinctive nature of the various sources. Many of our educational worries and problems, it seems to me, result from unconscious confusion in our programs and in our own minds of the separate purposes and characteristics of these several categories and domains. Quite succinctly, there are at least six different approaches available in designing and implementing various curricula: skill, data, concept, theme, attitude, process.

A skill curriculum could include any such educational activity or purpose as basic reading, auto mechanics, surgical technique, electronic repair, typing, stenography, cooking, penmanship, dressmaking, bricklaying, driving a car, carpentry, voice modulation and pacing, rope climbing, stagecraft, discus throwing, plowing, shrubbery pruning, basketball dribbling, tuba playing, hairdressing, leather tooling. There is no doubt that certain skills can be sophisticated into arts by some practitioners, but such sophistication usually represents a crossing from skill into one of the other five curricular domains, or it requires a certain mysterious egocentric or divinely inspired thrust within that practitioner that is not necessarily intrinsic in the skill itself.

Skill curriculum has some obvious advantages. It could prepare at least some people for the marketplace. The language or philos-

---

[1] The passage on "Whale Oil and Woodrow Wilson" first appeared under the author's byline in *Trend* 5, no. 3 (Spring 1969): 17, and is used here by permission.

ophy major could no longer blame schooling in general for the fact that he is ill-equipped with specific job skills upon his graduation; he would simply know that in choosing a language or philosophy major, he had clearly followed the wrong kind of curriculum if his major interest was preparation to fill a job that required certain skills. A course of study built solidly around the development of reading skill and unhindered by time limitations and the necessity to place students into classes would all but guarantee literacy in a given segment of the population.

Disadvantages are just as obvious. There are now some 20,000 distinct job categories in the United States, each no doubt involving certain skills, some general among several different jobs, some most likely quite peculiar to particular jobs. How could any educational institution train people in all those skills, especially when one considers the tremendous cost of the necessary equipment and material in light of the relatively small number of people who will enter any one job category. Consider the extreme unlikelihood of a young person's choosing a particular job and staying with it for the rest of his life. Furthermore, an exclusively skill curriculum could produce an individual terribly narrowed in his specialization and limited in his realization of those broad goals of education named earlier in this book: heightened awareness of life, exchange of knowledge, development of wisdom.

A *data curriculum* is the one most familiar to most of us. Its major purpose and procedure is the dissemination of information, even though some people try to mask that information under some such umbrella as "culture" or "knowledge" or "science" or even "education." Some single-cell samples of its content: *Julius Caesar*, Walt Whitman's life, the periodic chart, major causes of the Civil War, kings and queens of England, identification of African tribes, elements in water, who was Galileo, memorization of the Preamble to the Constitution, characteristics of metaphysical poetry, dates of the French Revolution, three kinds of stream, all Gaul is divided into how many parts.

The huge advantage of a data curriculum is that the massive investment in books and other educational materials and tools now in national inventory will not be jeopardized if the data curriculum is continued. Such a curriculum is also very teachable and quite testable—at least on the surface. Simple recall is all that it requires in its purest form. Data curriculum can also be very useful, as when the surgeon does indeed know that the troublesome appendix is likely to be in the lower right abdomen rather than the upper left neck. Let him be guided toward skill in handling the knife, but also give him data about where to cut with it.

Its disadvantages make us a bit more uncomfortable. How does who select from the limitless mountain of mankind's data collection what should be formally disseminated in the schools and what should not be? How does a school keep current with all the data in the midst of a knowledge explosion like that of our time—when some knowledge becomes obsolete before it can be reported to those in the world at large who are interested in it and when knowledge proliferates so rapidly that if a research chemist, for instance, were to do nothing at all for twenty-four hours every day but read the latest publications in his specialty, he would fall steadily behind the pace of that published growth in knowledge? How difficult is it to select from the mountain of data those pieces that will be meaningful' to whichever individual student is to be exposed to it?

The notion of *concept curriculum* probably develops in the face of the impossible dimensions and demands of the data curriculum. We can arrive at a concept curriculum very early in the study of literature, for instance, especially with the growing availability of paperbacks and of multimedia resources. Given: The individual reading levels of my fifty eleventh graders range from fourth through sixteenth. Given: It is unlikely that I can identify one book in which they will all be interested, and it is completely unrealistic to think that I can identify one book that they will all be able and willing to read well, given that range in abilities. Given: It is unlikely that I will be able to interest some of them in reading a book at all. Given: There are certain universal ideas or concepts that by definition of universality play some role in everyone's life—tragedy, for instance, or irony or faith or liberalism or power or reverence. I decide to develop a curricular unit around tragedy. Various instructional techniques can be utilized, even simultaneously within the fifty students: class discussion, buzz group, writing project, problem solving, etc.—perhaps enough different techniques so that a student might choose from among them. Various titles and kinds of communication—again, hopefully by choice of individual students—become the "devices" by which the concept can be approached or entered or explored as a class by the individuals being "taught." Some such "devices": a copy of *Macbeth*, a film of *Romeo and Juliet*, a synopsis of the Faust legend, filmstrips of the Oedipus cycle, a recording of *Death of a Salesman*, an account of Dreiser's *An American Tragedy*, with or without a reading of it, and a panel report on Aristotle's definition of tragedy.

If one were to go about developing a spiral curriculum as Bruner defined such a curriculum, he might find early success by making it basically a concept curriculum. There are elements of tragedy in *Chicken Little* as well as in *Lord of the Flies*, of social injustice in *Cinderella* as well as in *The Grapes of Wrath*, of satire in "Georgie-Porgie" as well as in *Animal Farm*. If one were to strive for an "interdisciplinary" curriculum, he might well try to achieve it through developing a concept curriculum. Pollution as a concept or phenomenon is in the distinct domain of which department: public health, science, social studies, philosophy, humanities, management, conservation, medicine, government? Doesn't its study allow a neat excuse for decategorizing the structure and organization of the typical campus? Certainly almost every traditional subject area that can be named has a huge reservoir of basic concepts underlying it which it can identify and verbalize as the foundations of the curriculum. Probably all the data traditionally associated with that subject area is but device or vehicle or language for making one aware, eventually, of basic concepts. Unfortunately, in the recent past, the persistence of and reverence for particular vehicles has smothered the basic concepts they are supposed to illustrate. A data study of Heraclitus, Hegel, and Hoffer has replaced philosophy, for instance, just as surely as people will tell you in all sobriety that they knew nothing of gravity until they learned about Isaac Newton and his apple. In how many mathematics classes has working through an endless array of problems replaced the revelation of a series of basic concepts about measurements and proportion and shape and arrangement and logic and the like?

Concept curriculum, handled well, could go far toward developing at least the first two ideals of education as listed earlier: heightened awareness of life and exchange of knowledge.

A *theme curriculum* is quite similar both to concept curriculum and to attitude curriculum, it seems to me, except that it is flavored rather heavily with the particular culture that produces it—much more so than the concept curriculum, which tends to be based on more purely rational and abstract notions. But, it is so flavored less blatantly and purposely than the attitude curriculum, which tends toward almost pure propaganda, no matter how lofty or laudable the slant or attitude. A sample theme curriculum might be centered around the Dignity of Man, for instance, and such a theme connotes and assumes far more than such a simplistically pure notion as dignity alone, or tragedy, or satire, or power. Theme curriculum offers all the pedagogical advantages of concept curriculum, with less of its objectivity and abstraction. God and Man, Order in the Universe, Creation and Re-creation, Equality and Brotherhood of Man, Homemaking as Fulfillment of Self, Evolution of Government, Comparative Religion, Magnificence of Nature, Measurement and Man—curricula in every discipline could be designed and taught for thematic purposes, but everyone presupposes certain fundamental stances or beliefs or senses of direction as surely as does "the glory that was Greece and the grandeur that was Rome." It is the presence of such presupposition that distinguishes theme curriculum from concept curriculum.

It is to a great extent the *degree* of the presence of such presupposition and assumption and connotation that sets the *attitude curriculum* apart from the theme curriculum. The most extreme and open example of an attitude curriculum I have ever heard was described to me by the founder of a program for ghetto girls in a metropolitan public high school.

"That school was the epitome of everything that could go wrong with American society and education," he reported. "The school was located in a neighborhood of whorehouses and run-down bars. It was likely that a girl would drop out to bear a child long before she would graduate. The school consistently held the highest student dropout rate in the city and the greatest turnover of teachers.

"We determined to accomplish one goal if no other with those girls. There was little question that they would become mothers in no time at all. That was only a matter of weeks or months for a good many of them. So we determined that they would become mothers who would nurture in their own children the idea that school wasn't really such a bad place to go. We simply wanted to affect their attitudes so that they in turn would influence the attitudes of the next generation of students—their children—who would come into the schools."

That report capsulizes a positive approach toward developing a curriculum whose main purpose is to shape attitude. From a negative point of view, I wonder how many attitudes our traditional curricula and practices have shaped. How many negative attitudes, even negative skills, have been learned while we educators have thought we have been up to something altogether different in the schools? We like to think that we have been teaching and that our students have been learning pretty much whatever we eventually allow to show up in our quizzes and on our final examinations. How much do students simultaneously learn to despise, to cheat, to lie, to "play the game" called school, to "psych out" teachers, to manipulate exam results and teacher behavior, to become cynical and devious and miserable and angry?

It would be interesting to be able to determine such secondary and unintentional results of our curriculum and instruction, then to line them up one by one with the "positive" results of our stated primary mission, and to see which outstrips which in magnitude and lasting effect. The timeless stereotypes of "school" and of "teaching"—whether wardens, welts, and work or simps, saps, and silliness—may be the most valid indicators of the pedagogical effectiveness of our schools up to now.

At any rate, that attitudes can be shaped by schooling is of no question. Of what use we can or will or should make of that fact has not yet been determined or even recognized in most attempts at curriculum development—in considerations of what we are up to and why. A botany lecturer set on establishing reverence for life in his students or appreciation of patterns in nature might well scrap the usual data curriculum in the course of study and proceed by whatever means are most effective to nurture those attitudes (hardly the lecture, unless he is a spellbinder). I refer again to one of the reasons I became an English teacher—because of an attitude exemplified by one particular English teacher—or to my flirtation with geology because of attitudes exuded by certain instructors. Many of the major results of my own formal education as I think back are far more attitudinal than data, certainly, or even than conceptual or thematic. I remember and emulate the sense of humor of a high school physics instructor, the competence and self-confidence of a graduate instructor in psychology, the grace and kindness of a literature professor, the craftsmanship of a radio technician, the love for liberty of a French teacher, the showmanship of a classical scholar, the dynamics of a critic and teacher of the humanities, the quiet precision and composure of a poet-teacher I knew. All these results I can articulate have to do more with attitude than with anything else in education. I cannot carve the *Pieta* nor give you its dates or dimensions nor what conviction might have impelled its creator to sculpt it in the first place. But, because of something in my education, I respect it, admire it, wonder at it, and even participate in it. That something has to do with an attitude.

Process curriculum is open to the same abuse or misinterpretation or mal-implementation that four of the other five kinds of curricula suggested here are probably open to. In short, every one of them can be turned into a data curriculum and probably will be by that huge army of educators who are so long and so deeply immersed in the pile, who are so much product and partisan of the usual, the customary, the traditional that they fail not only to acknowledge, understand, and accept the novel, the unorthodox, the innovative; they fail also to recognize their own stable, conservative, unmoving, unaware positions. They fail to recognize just how long and how deeply they are part of the traditional pile. Some of them even think they are themselves indeed unusual, adventurous, daring, and innovative in their beliefs and practices. Can you find an educator in the country who will tell you that his school program is not "student centered"? Can you find one who will say, "Yes, most of the pedagogical techniques practiced in my school are right up-to-date with the middle of the nineteenth century"?

At any rate, there will probably always be "learning" as opposed to "learning about," and no matter what they say they are up to, most educators will have their students "learning about." It is a phenomenon as much an unshakable part of our heritage as original sin, I am convinced. For instance, linguistic scholars for decades have demonstrated that youngsters have the "sentence form" and other basic structural patterns of their native languages well in their psychological makeups by age three or thereabouts. Yet teachers still think they are introducing "the sentence" at age seven or eight, and they complain that some kids have not yet "learned" it by high school or college. Those teachers are concerned not with a student's *learning the sentence* but with his *learning about* the sentence (a particular kind of sentence, by the way, which may not be elemental to that student's "native language" or dialect). Data curriculum is given massively to *learning about*. *Learning*, as used here, is given to assimilation, to participation, to practice and example—with or without the student's ability to verbalize what he has learned. *Learning about* is more easily tested by recall—the most common kind of evaluation used in our schools. *Learning*, as used here, is not so easily measured by the typical schoolman's usual techniques, and that makes a lot of us educators and parents nervous. "How will I know what the kid has learned—that he's gotten anywhere?" I am not sure we can do a good job of determining such things by traditional means of recall examination. We only make ourselves believe that through his test results we know what he has learned and that that learning represents his having "gotten somewhere."

In such a context of both conscious and unconscious conservatism and because of the gargantuan hold that data curriculum has on the nation's schools and on the minds of its schoolmen, two kinds of process curricula will undoubtedly develop, both called "process curricula" but different from each other: (1) a process curriculum in which practice and preachment are largely indistinguishable from each other, (2) a data curriculum in which students will learn about process curriculum. Anyone who has listened to endless lectures on the evils and ineffectiveness of lecturing as an instructional technique for most teachers knows how swiftly and uncompromisingly a non-data approach can be turned into the Mr. Hyde of data presentation.

The broadest kind of process curriculum would be one in which the student simply learned how to learn and proceeded to do so from beginning to end of "course" or "education." Data or device would become tools or language for the curriculum, but they would not necessarily need to be the same data or device for everyone, especially since individuals probably develop learning styles peculiar to themselves. If a more specialized process curriculum were to be built—say, a curriculum built around *symbolic process*—it would seem obvious that certain kinds of data might be used more efficiently and effectively than certain other kinds. Language as symbolic process would obviously work well in such a specialized process curriculum as would certain elements of religion and ritual, of mathematics, of scientific theory, of advertising, of clinical psychology. A curriculum is *synthetic process* might use experience from those subject areas we now think of as chemistry, woodcarving, drama, ceramics, poetry, musical composition, design, architecture, esperanto.

Process curriculum on smaller scale or in less abstract process might be built of inquiry or translation (in general—not just linguistic translation) or metamorphosis or assembly-line production or regeneration or echo or milling or refining or induction and deduction or certain kinds of behavior—democracy, literality, degeneration, brainstorming, group dynamics.

It can be seen, from these few examples at least, that processes often become manifest in or require the skill of their practitioners. But the process has to do more with abstract principle, with the generalizable law or fact lying behind the fingertip practice that is the normal province of the skill curriculum.

Obviously, there are overlaps among these six kinds of curricula. Obviously, all six are at work, as I suggested earlier, in typical school programs right now. Just as obviously, we are not always aware that they are at work, nor are we always willing to acknowledge that all six are legitimate foundations for curriculum —each in its own right a sound base from which to build school programs, to select materials and experiences, and to shape educa-

tional practices. The data curriculum and its typical recall examination have so pervaded our educational souls that we feel guilty
if there are no facts with which to write a test at the end of the
course. We find students who love school, for a change, but
"haven't learned anything"—except to love school—and that really
bothers us! We tremble a bit at not being able, for instance, to
"measure attitudes—you cannot test them!" when motivational
research and opinion polls provide thumbrules of the day in government and politics, business and industry. For all their headline-
making errors and all the academic snobbery that greets them, such
polls and such "popular" research are probably no less accurate at
measuring fantastically chimerical variables than the typical classroom exam is at measuring what a student knows. And they certainly offer more accurate means of measuring how a student feels
or what he believes. We shut from our minds the suggestion that
education is not really in the business of testing at all but in the
business of learning—that eventually it is the "student" who knows
what he knows. Will we openly grant him that responsibility
which is already by nature of the human beast *his*, although so
many of us educators and parents think we can somehow climb
inside his skin and tell him what he is or is not, what he knows or
does not, how he feels or does not? If that is possible, what a
directionless, soulless sack of flesh that student has been. If we were
more interested in learning than in certification, in institutional
service to the responsible individual rather than institutional control, we might consider openly allowing the student what he
already has in surreptitious truth: his own best measure of himself,
uncomfortable as that truth is for many individuals.

Obviously, there are overlaps among these six different curricular purposes, but rather than recognizing them and building our
programs from the pluralism and diversity they systematically represent, we let the English teacher, saturated with literary appreciation, lock in deadly and unnecessary warfare with the Typing
teacher, thoroughly rooted in the skills of preparing the business
letter. So the two smolder in their separate corners and condemn
each other's scholastic programs as groundless, with their students
often caught helpless and embarrassed and confused in the middle
of the arena until the principal comes up with some patchy entente
—an ineffectual hybrid like Business English, or in other scholastic

combat zones, with Vocational Science or Academic Woodshop or General Math. (I had an elementary vocal music teacher who always designated certain members of our gang to be "listeners" during the compulsory music class. A fine compromise indeed!) Often such hybrid labels are euphemisms for "lower standards of quality or expectation."

Why don't we quit making excuses for the presence and legitimacy in our schools of the five kinds of curricula other than data? Can we give up some of the overwhelming fetishism for exclusively data curriculum, a preoccupation that so often makes hypocrites and drudges and shortsighted creatures of us all? Must we equate high quality in education only with higher and deeper data curricula.

I remember Tim Siever walking into my classroom one evening after dismissal. Straight-A senior, he was the dull but pure and perfect product of our data curriculum. And, as typical after school recreation, he was at the moment extending himself in a collected volume of Ripley's *Believe It or Not*.

"Just listen to this, Mr. Kline," he began, then ripped off some weird fragment of exotica from the volume. "Isn't that interesting? Here's another one."

And off it came, another weirdo. And a third, and a fourth—until my temples could take no more of the siege.

"Tim," I began, "look out that window. Look at that lowering sun out there. Isn't that interesting? You know what? It's there every evening—even on cloudy days—and in the morning it's somewhere else, and at noon, too—never, *never* with the sky looking exactly the same around it, though. Isn't that interesting? And, have you taken a look, lately, at Jennie—at Jennie, who sits beside you in class—Jennie with the marvelous legs and marvelous eyes? Isn't she interesting? Or will she never replace Ripley? God bless you, tiny Tim, because I can't."

Truthfully, I wanted to say all this, but I did not get off more than the first sentence or two. Instead, I mumbled into my pile of papers, stapled a couple of them together, Tim folded Ripley under his arm, and we parted silently.

5

"For Once, Then, Something"—
Four Structures and Humanity

Others taunt me with having knelt at well-curbs
Always wrong to the light, so never seeing
Deeper down in the well than where the water
Gives me back in a shining surface picture
Me myself in the summer heaven, godlike,
Looking out of a wreath of fern and cloud puffs.
Once, when trying with chin against a well-curb,
I discerned, as I thought, beyond the picture,
Through the picture, a something white, uncertain,
Something more of the depths—and then I lost it.
Water came to rebuke the too clear water.
One drop fell from a fern, and lo, a ripple
Shook whatever it was lay there at bottom,
Blurred it, blotted it out. What was that whiteness?
Truth? A pebble of quartz? For once, then, something.[1]

—*Robert Frost*

At least for purposes of this discussion or inquiry, there is no
hierarchy among the six kinds of curricula catalogued in the last
chapter. There is no distinction one from the other by weight or
by value. All are equally legitimate, equally valid, equally viable—
at least for discussion here. If there is movement or progression
among them, it is circular so that none of the six comes "first" or
"last"; for by now mankind is so far into civilization that arguing
over which should be given prominence over the other—skill or
data, for instance, or concept or process—is a very, very academic
argument. If the end of education is wisdom or maturity as a human being or a heightened awareness of life and if one of its major

---

[1] "For Once, Then, Something," from *The Poetry of Robert Frost* edited by
Edward Connery Lathem, p. 276. Copyright 1923, 1928, 1934, 1949, © 1969
by Holt, Rinehart and Winston, Inc. Copyright 1951, © 1956, 1962 by Robert
Frost. Reprinted by permission of Holt, Rinehart and Winston, Inc.

activities is the exchange of knowledge, the devotees of that curriculum that is heavily oriented toward development of vocational skills, say, must recognize that job training, crucial as it might be to the man without a job in a society which places premium on employment, is only a means toward survival, not necessarily a satisfactory reason for living. By the same token, defenders of the data curriculum must recognize that simple accumulation of verbalized knowledge does not guarantee development of attitudes nor of skills. Those who would push heavily for process curriculum need to recognize that process without substance is like a wind tunnel without wind. And so forth.

If we are to seek hierarchy or movement or development that will elucidate our quest for more meaningful structures of education, we might more pertinently turn to considering the development of the individual human being. It begins life as a simple organism, then learns to perceive those things that it then learns to represent in language, language by which it participates in humanity, and then develops whatever it eventually recognizes as meaningful in life—meaningful even as absurdity or chaos at last can be defined. Until we take this distinctive development of humanity into consideration, until we recognize and satisfy the need for such a broad philosophical base, we will spend a great deal of time shooting from the hip or hopping from headline to headline in our quest for ideal education. Until we touch this fundamental process of human development, we will be unable to take more than wild guesses at what it might be necessary for a person to know, for instance, or at how we might best go about educating ourselves. Ask an educator to give you the philosophical base behind his school program—an educator who has not self-consciously reappraised his own basic development as an individual human being—and he will tick off those clichés about "whole child" and "individualized instruction" and "meeting the needs of youth" and "freedom within structure" and the rest that clutter every school manual in the country like cut flowers—and with about as much depth of root and syrup of life to them, too.

One evening a year or two ago, my son observed what I suppose every child in the age of motorized speed has observed. We were driving along a country road near home when he said, "Look, Daddy, the moon is riding along with us."

Now my first impulse, being dutiful father and conscientious teacher, was to say what was said to me when I was his age and to just about every other kid who has ever looked out a car window and "seen the moon travelling along with us": "No, son, it only looks as if the moon is travelling along with us. Actually, we are moving . . . ," etc., etc., the basis for which is the belief that the separate, simple perceptions of every person who has ever looked out from a moving vehicle and "seen the moon travelling along with us" are indeed erroneous simply because they happen not to fit into a logical system that most of us have agreed "makes sense"—laws of motion, relative points of view, etc.

So I bit my tongue and said, "Yeah, how about that!"

But the story does not end there. It was that time in spring when winter wheat in our part of the country was out of the ground a good three or four inches—high enough to pepper the fields which I drove by each day with countless points of reference. So, since the country roads on my way to school were not too heavily travelled, I took to checking my own perceptions. The weeds and trees and roadside immediately outside the car as I drove along appeared, obviously, to be moving in a direction opposite that of the movement of the car. Distant objects—trees, hillsides, certain farm buildings—appeared to be moving with the car. Logically, there must be some point in between where things appear to stand still—on either side of the car. With enough patience, enough luck with minimal traffic, and enough winter wheat sprouts to serve as an endless array of focal points, I eventually identified that position of motionlessness, and no one can now convince me that the universe that surrounds me when I am driving a car is not moving in two swirling, somewhat oval planes, the left one clockwise, the right one counterclockwise, with a confluence approaching me from straight ahead.

I know, in that way lies madness. I know—reinforce such generalization of gross perception in a child, and he will not only march to a different drum, he will likely be drummed out of circulation. I know. What difference does it all make anyhow, many ask. I know all those reactions and remarks. I have made them myself many times.

My point is to question whether or not Copernicus (or Ptolemy before him) would have had a chance in the typical contemporary educational institution. I wonder if he would ever have "gotten off the ground," as we slang it. Or to come off the rare example, to question whether our schooling encourages—even allows—its students to move on more primitive levels of natural development as a human being as well as on the race's most sophisticated level. Do we make it likely that a child will move on a more primary level than the cultural, the generally acceptable level of what most of us say is logical or sensible? Do we recognize the complexity and relativity, the shortcomings and limitations and private nature of language—its capacity for error as well as its advantages and possibilities for communication and its control of all culture, perhaps its shaping of all knowledge and thinking? Do we urge the child to perceive as well as he can for himself, and to report as accurately as he can what he perceives? If the perception differs from our own, do we reinforce trust in his own perceptions, or do we, like most of the chemistry teachers I have ever known, simply tell him he is wrong when his classroom "experiment" (what a misnomer for *procedural exercise*) turns out some kind of blue liquid rather than the red solid that was supposed to result, according to the lab manual? Do we want a child to listen to his own blood run, to feel the rush of wind in his throat, to tremble with nerve end and muscle tone, and to begin his perceptions from there?

I think not, obviously, by the tone of my question. Rather, we proliferate a skim-top curriculum that ignores all but the most surface manifestations of man's development to date. We brush the bubbles off the immediate surface of the whole magnificent movement of mankind up from curious brine, smear them broadside over a slab called education, then wonder why in their thinness they fail to satisfy, why they pop and dry up under the eyes of students we bring to look at them as what *we* have decided God hath wrought. Darwinian biology, after all, will someday seem as quaint as Icarian flight, astrophysics as folksy and old hat as witchcraft, biochemistry as outdated as cave painting. Hemingway is the next millenium's minor writer of the late Christian Era, known only to a few scholars of the tongue who are acquainted with the intricacies of twentieth-century English. I remember a big deal some teacher made somewhere in my schooling over the difference between *post card* and *postal card*, and I guess we were supposed to believe that life would end if we were not able to distinguish between the two her way. I have yet to conduct business in either post office or five-and-ten-cent store with any confusion about the two terms. Do you know—can you believe—that one of the requirements for earning the doctorate at some of our universities is that the candidate type his dissertation on twenty-pound bond paper? How's that for encouraging the student to listen to his own blood run before he sets out to check some perceptions about the world around him?

Man is an *organism* capable of physical *perceptions* upon which he builds *language* by which he creates and communicates meaningful *life* or culture or civilization—by which he lives and moves and has his being. And that highest level of development includes and leads to all kinds of things: reasons for being, ethics, beliefs, mystery, behavior, fact, values, science, religion, history, laziness, literature, music, revolution, art, innovation, alternatives, love, hate, anger, power, action, passivity, poetry, total bags, even nit-picking. We will not argue whether emotion is an attribute of man as organism or as learner; it is obvious that complete man is capable of emotion. Nor will we enter the traditional feud between hereditarians and environmentalists. However he gets here, man is. And he is in such variety and number and degree that his study offers plenty of material for our purposes.

Simultaneously and equally important, the four phases of development (because, as a basic assumption, that is what they are or at least that is what my own philosophy at the moment guides me to say they are)—exist or develop not just as separate phases of sophistication in the life of a single human being. It is also true that an earlier phase accumulates in part in the development of at least a portion of each following phase. Man as organism helps to determine the nature and ability of man as perceiver. Both man as organism and man as perceiver help to determine the nature and capability of the language man develops. All three—organism, perception, language—accumulate in part in one segment of the level of *life as lived*. Graphically:

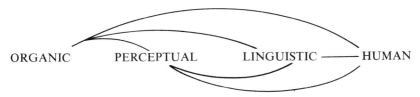

ORGANIC   PERCEPTUAL   LINGUISTIC ——— HUMAN

The really startling significance of man's creation of life in a test tube is the realignment of these phases and the possible consequences of that realignment. Man might literally play God, from the point of view of those who subscribe to St. John's idea that "In the beginning was the *Logos*." The development might move full circle with man's capability to create organisms that can develop humanly.

Now, let me define *intelligence* as the degree to which a person tunes in on any or all of the four phases of development we have identified. A person might be more organically intelligent, for instance, than he is linguistically intelligent. Or he might be more perceptually and linguistically intelligent than he is organically and philosophically. And so on. My language, occasionally, can get rather earthy in describing the person who seems intelligent purely and solely on an organic level.

Next, I could define *education* as the manifest integration of these four phases, certainly as such integration could lead to a heightened awareness of life, that would lead, I would hope, to the development of wisdom. The most fully educated person is the person who is extremely intelligent in all four phases to the extent that balance and merger take place among the four phases in his life, and he finds it unnecessary or impossible to be constantly aware that each is at least in part a phase unto itself within his life.

What has happened in schooling as most of us have seen it practiced and as we ourselves have practiced it? (I am tempted to say perpetrated rather than practiced.) As collective or total man has evolved and proliferated along a model like the four-phase one described above, with an imponderable number of variations in degree and kind of development, all sorts of stuff has piled up, spilled over, been crushed, piled on, pushed over, pulled down, piled higher and deeper. Some of that stuff has been skimmed off or pulled out or picked up and made into a culture, some of it into a different culture, some into a third culture, etc., etc. Some has been made into value systems, etc., etc. Some into etc., etc. And, lo! There in P.S. 999, we have still another bundle of it, and this bundle is known as "The Curriculum of P.S. 999," complete with lesson plans, quizzes, and supplementary programmed texts (available at your regional mail order distribution point, School Supplies, Unlimited, Inc., $1.98 per set).

What bothers me about all this, I guess, is that we teach a bundle of stuff that a whole lot of us think we believe in, but we think we believe in it without ever having rechecked the philosophy which has produced it, without ever having rechecked the language by which the philosophy that produced the stuff was enabled to come into existence, without ever having rechecked the perceptions by which the language was developed by which the philosophy that produced the stuff was enabled to come into existence, without ever having rechecked the organism that made the perceptions by which the language was developed by which the philosophy that produced the stuff was enabled to come into existence. And, we teach the stuff so damned dogmatically and smugly! We play the priest unshaven and shorn without ever recognizing that there just might be some value in checking the original house that Jack built! I do not mind anyone playing priest, so long as the kid he is "educating" is led to recognize the wellspring plus the process of development which has been the source of whatever the priest is passing off as gospel. Let the kid touch wellspring and process and decide for himself.

I could quote Frost on education (for the ten thousandth time): "Let them pile the bricks in on me, but let me build with them for myself."

I could quote Thoreau (or, more likely, misquote him): "The man who seems to be out of step may not be out of step at all. He may simply be marching to the beat of a different drum."

I *could* even quote Christ: "The kingdom of God is within you."

But, maybe that is too big a leap to leap right now. Simply stated: Can we develop a curriculum that moves on all four phases and does so honestly, not tokenly—and if not a curriculum, then some mechanism which allows that to happen? Can we cultivate an educational approach that at least does not force some kid to spit back to a teacher those perceptions and that language that reflect some philosophy or lifeview that that little organism has not been allowed, in as large a measure as possible, to develop for himself?

If nothing else results from our addressing ourselves to such questions, we might share development of, or movement toward, new points in thought and perception, which in turn might result in a genuinely new program in a school. More hopefully, we might in the process enter new areas of inquiry, might develop new frames of reference that will lead us to genuine discoveries on a unique frontier: man's ability to dream and think and feel, both as an individual and as a social being. Or, if we end up only where we have been up to now, we will at least have some idea of how we got there and why we are there.

At this point, I am ready to suggest a basis for curriculum, one that I myself have dreamed up in rather vague, intuitive ways, and to offer it up for circumspection—hopeful circumspection. I would like to see if we could build a curriculum from Unity, Diversity, Process, and Substance—not simply reorganize what we are now doing in the schools into these four classifications but, beginning with those four as desirable assumed bases as the fundamentals of life and universe and humanity, see what we can create and whether or not they are comprehensive. In a sense, you see, we are at a more sophisticated level than the ancient Greeks' Earth, Air, Fire, and Water, for two, maybe three, or all four of our elements are abstractions; but I would accept them, I think, as comprehensively as the Greeks took their division of the known. I am reasonably sure, at least, that these four abstractions—Unity, Diversity, Process, Substance—include all the elements of my personal lifeview in its entirety at this time.

I do not want merely to force reconsideration and perhaps reshuffling of what is already extant, although I do not mind generating excitement from mutual attempts at such reorganization and from the freshness of previously untried points of view. Furthermore, with the acceptance of my proposed curricular foundation—Unity, Diversity, Process, Substance—I might merely succeed in selling "Kline" under the label of "curriculum," and that is the kind of selling, on a larger market and by a larger collective mindset or lifeview, that I am not sure I like. At best, it can lead to exciting schooling, but in the final analysis, it remains propaganda and direction rather than total education. If education is to move on the level of organism as well as of the other three phases described earlier, genuine discovery by an individual learner is probably the primary requirement. Yet, I am myself almost ready to believe that the four elements I have named are the basic structures of life as life has developed from collective language, perception, organism—that the four are (hopefully) much bigger than mere Kline.

But first we need to consider language—that level of development that strikes me as most distinctively man's, that allows him, in turn, to develop humanity. For labels—this whole phenomenon of language—will be our major barrier, perhaps, since language is at once not only the means by which we communicate but also the means by which we can misunderstand and be misunderstood. A hit in the mouth is a hit in the mouth, but in how many different ways can the word *love* be spoken, written, heard, interpreted, translated into action or inaction? Labels! How difficult it is to find words that will take fellow conversationalists to the bedrock I want us to explore. What has been said so far seems bland to me only because certain truths that are verbalized in it are so easily verbalized but so rarely or never practiced. Dewey might have suffered the quiet crucifixion of being misunderstood—by friends as by enemies. *Humanity* is perhaps not the exact word to name the fourth phase of man's development, but the exact word is simply not available when the idea is, so I leap on the nearest approximation that immediate language offers—mainly because of impatience at searching for the exact word or unwillingness to coin a new one.

And, I certainly did not intend by listing four levels or phases—organism, perception, language, humanity—that we would then proceed to "teach" those four phases, that all students would then learn to identify and describe *organism, perception, language, humanity* and to classify all knowledge, all life, under those four labels—*learning about*, once again, rather than living. I cannot at this point really tell what the curriculum looks like that might lead to education as I hope education to be. Indeed, there might not be a "curriculum." Probably, the individual student will need at least in part to develop his own curriculum. I suspect that the eventual "course of study" will turn out to be a list of no substantives at all; rather, it will describe a style, perhaps, an approach, a role or series of roles, for the learner and for the "teacher." Rather, it will describe a guide for "teacher" behavior, for I suspect at least one criterion at this point: I want little or no "teaching" in the process at all; I want nothing but learning. The first "instructional behavior" I want to see in the teacher-student relationship is the "teacher's" honest, full attempt to learn where the student is in the student's world and what that world is like. I hope the "teacher" will remain in such a learning role throughout the duration of the relationship, whether or not he develops other roles along the way.

But, see? Already I am using language that we have heard before, that we have heard and nodded to in agreement—nodded to, then violated its intent by our own actions. I suppose that leads me to a second criterion for the process of education I would like to see dreamed up and developed: there shall be no unforced violation of ideal; rather, there shall be an unyielding loyalty to ideal— unyielding until the impasse of ultimate frustration is reached.

Beyond these two statements, I hesitate to verbalize at the present stage of this inquiry for fear of becoming entirely despotic in imposing my lifeview on the process I hope we will design. There are, after all, certain notions I would like at least to read into the record for now. If I allowed myself further zeal, I would stamp them to the page as dogma. For instance, a fourth-grader's comment to friend Donald Waldera during an interview prompted me to like very much the accommodation of privacy for the student in school. In helping list what school should be like, the youngster simply asked for a place where he could be alone when he felt the need to be alone during the school day. Right now, I believe that a guarantee of some measure of privacy—physical privacy—should be an absolute requirement in any school program we design. But maybe I am simply swayed momentarily by freshness and enthusiasm for the thought of a fourth grader.

Like many others, I have said that every teacher is sooner or later a teacher of language—a teacher of reading, of speaking, of writing. Like others, I have been accused of wanting to shirk my duty as English teacher, to have teachers in other departments "do the job" on the kids that I should be doing. Yet, my accusers would gaily have me read the term papers they assign in their courses—"You read it for mechanics and style, and I'll read it for content." I know what they mean, but I bait them by pretending I do not—sometimes just to hear them sputter but, more often and more hopefully, to urge them toward two considerations: (1) It is at last impossible to divorce "language" from "content." (2) Language is not simply the superficial handmaiden of everything else that is somehow supposed to be more substantive; language is the basis of all things human, including whatever "course of study" my accuser might think he has in his personal custody. It is the phenomenon, the symbolic process, the universal means that cuts across or underlies all six approaches to curriculum: skill, data, concept, theme, attitude, process. It is in such a sense—obvious truth, to me—that I consider all teachers to be teachers of language and that I consider all curriculum, all life, to be a linguistic phenomenon inasmuch as it is more than anything else our language that sets us apart in creation as humanity and that enables us to practice what we have come to call human life. Value systems differ, beliefs differ, bodies of knowledge differ, but the process and historical and developmental nature of language are as common to human experience as life itself. Yes, there are differences among languages, but linguistic process is common—and who knows, maybe there once was a single human language, a la Babel's story, though I would not push the possibility here.

All language is metaphor, and metaphor something much more pervasive and fundamental to human development than some little freak of comparison that some tricky poet has used to spice up a prosy statement in a poem so that English teachers can set their kids baldly to hunting it out like a nugget of iron pyrite. In order to be recognized as language or as metaphor, lines of script or of print must represent something other than themselves. So must bursts of air, controlled by larynx, lips, tongue, teeth, represent ideas or things before we are willing to call them language. The sequence of language development—experience, listening, speaking, reading, writing—reflects the symbolic process of language. We feel or see or do before we hear "words," we hear a sound before we first speak it, we know a word orally before we learn to read it, and we read it before we can spell it, at least in our early years. That sequence is built on the fact that one level of language development depends on an earlier one for sense or meaning and that all meaning is rooted primarily in experience—through the sensory perceptions of the organism that are then associated with sounds— even though most of us eventually reach a level of sophistication that might be called "linguistic experience." Man has certainly reached such an advanced stage in his collective development; that is, certain men have arrived there, where language builds language and we can talk about talk or handle abstractions that have no direct roots in sensory experience.

Consideration of language as symbolic process leads sooner or later to the onomatopoetic theory of the origin of language—that words developed as oral imitations of physical reality. And I do not really care which scholars have or have not debunked the whole theory. I accept it as a useful idea, whether I need satisfy the rigorous demands of others by calling it a myth or not. I can accept it as validly as I have used *Hansel and Gretel, The House that Jack Built,* and *Cinderella* elsewhere in this book and as handily as I would invent God if someone naggingly demonstrated beyond reproof and undeniably that God did not exist. That, too, is one of the facts of language: in a sense, saying makes it so, although I realize that calling a cliff not a cliff but a highway and thus walking over it to one's surprise and ultimate conclusion is an everpresent reality also.

But to the development of language as symbolic process and the onomatopoetic theory in particular: The Indo-European root *agh* or *ang* sounds remarkably like the choking or strangling noise that is employed or implied in any of the actions or situations—the "meanings"—that lie behind English words in which the *agh* or *ang* roots are evident: strangle, wrangle, aghast, ghastly, anger, anguish, angle, hang. The physical fact of choking off, for one reason or another, is inherent in every word. *Mama,* or some sound similar to it, shows up with similar meaning in so many different languages, I like to believe, perhaps because *ah* is such a simple sound for the human mechanism to make and *mmm* can be sounded merely by closing the lips for *ah*. No wonder *mama* is one of the first "words" sounded by so many children. No wonder it so quickly becomes associated in the child's mind with the pleasure of food and comfort in the easing of hunger pains or the curing of the discomfort of dirty diapers.

The more abstract the language-symbol becomes (the further it moves from concrete reality), the greater chance of miscommunication. "My dog is dead" can hardly be misinterpreted as a statement of fact. "There is bitterness in her death" cries for additional statement, for supporting argument, for interpretation, for definition beyond the merely 1:1 correspondence of the phrase "my dead dog" with the concrete fact, sensorily documented, of a furry corpse lying on the ground.

Language as symbolic process leads ultimately to mystery, to the ultimate mystery of humanity itself. Whether it makes that mystery possible, creates it, or merely communicates its presence to us, I am not prepared to guess. I am ready to believe that language is simply a vehicle for communication, which may someday be replaced by a more efficient vehicle, until I read again the first page or two of *Moby Dick*; then, I sway toward language also as creator of mystery in human experience. At any rate, since we are biologically compelled to be social beings, and traditionally so inclined, we have had to agree somewhat on what each symbol represents before we have been able to recognize it as usable language. Without a system of correspondences (which is another way of describing language as symbolic process), consider what would not be available to man, or at best available only to a severely limited degree. Where would we be without our codes of morality, our ethical standards, our systems of values, our religious beliefs—the honor, glory, dignity, belief—the entire knowledge that mankind now holds as setting himself apart from the brutes? Without language, our history would be gone, our science gone, our dialogue impossible, our existence as a race of beings void of reason and meaning and belief.

To put myself in debt to Frost once more, he often said that a good poem begins in delight and ends in wisdom, that poetry is play on the brink of mystery. I doubt that he would object to our extending his definition to language, even as a classroom pursuit or procedure. One of the first steps toward language is the fascination of a child with his own gurgling and cooing and the fluttering of his own lips. Initiated in such physical, organic delight, his language develops through association of perceived reality with concurrent sound and through the eventual social awareness of verbal stimulus and response. Before he is done with life, that same child can learn to use language to call himself a Child of God or an Accident of Fate or a Product of Physical Phenomena, and through language he can grapple with Cause beyond Cause or Ground of Being or Existence before Essence. He categorizes knowledge into mathematics, science, social studies, and language, or life into Unity, Diversity, Process, and Substance. Through what language makes possible, he encounters the possibility that if there is perfect knowledge in the universe, it lies beyond man's comprehension; the de facto knowledge, for which we have found the symbols to communicate as human beings, might still appear to us as less than perfect, as magnificent and glorious error, perhaps infinite error, but error all the same. Error that puts the lie to human calendars by more or less one quarter of a day in each three hundred sixty-five. Error that sends the mathematician chasing after endless decimal points in pi. Error that keeps us human, wondering if the earth is speeding up or slowing down, if we live till death or die from birth, if ape or angel looms our dawning or our destiny. Error makes us human; to be human is to be imperfect, and that allows us to believe we are getting somewhere. And all because of language.

Yet, the miracle of this marvelous imperfection, this ultimate incommunication that we share and that we call our language, this symbolic process—the miracle of it is that by it we communicate: magnificent error keeping magnificent erring man ever in imperfect communion with himself, yearning to hear, yearning to sound that perfect word that, according to St. John, called the universe and this humanity into being. So much sound and cerebration in the error called language, and all of it uniquely man centered, seeming to make sense!

The teacher who accepts in all its richness and mystery the concept of language as symbolic process will not soon again, without strong personal reservation, say that English is something taught in the English classroom, but hardly in his own science or history or geography or fairytale, or quantitative analysis or Freudian psychology classroom. He will think twice, I hope, before he has his students, in the name of teaching a lesson in language, merely copy twenty single and "absolute" definitions to "this week's vocabulary list" of twenty polysyllabic phenomena culled from the lesser regions of our linguistic periphery. He will try to compromise the smugness and arrogance of that student or colleague who says, "I don't want you to answer my question with a deeper question. I want to know The One Right Answer that will close the matter forever in my mind!" Only with the greatest misgiving will he encourage that child who writes a dogmatic 200-word treatise on "Communism versus Democracy," the child believing she has thereby ended debate on the subject forever. Only with humility will he describe a system of grammar or logic or ethics or operational procedures or physics as a set of exhaustive and infallible rules.

Language as symbolic process is probably the most basic of structures, for nothing else in education would have been possible without it. It is also probably the most pervasive of structures. It provides the rationale for instruction in effective reporting, an art that demands foremost the accurate observation, through the five organic senses, of facts and surroundings and actions. Inquiry as technique or formal procedure is but built along the developmental linguistic model of survey or perception, of focus, of definition, of generalization, and eventually of refinement or reinforcement. Race hatred—and any prejudice or intransigence in humanity—is but a manifestation of the linguistic phenomenon of stereotype. Language as process—or its pursuit and study—enlightens the way to effective argument in mandating precision of statement. It provides insight into penchants of style as well as predilections in philosophy when, for instance, the abstract value judgments in the diction of *Silas Marner* are contrasted with the clinical word choices in *A Farewell to Arms*. It enables the close reader to learn why the calculated duplicity of a great poem is always infinitely greater than any prose paraphrase of that poem can be, why definitive meaning always lies somewhere beyond the cloture of debate on any topic worth pondering.

And, of course, language as symbolic process serves as a subject for endless contemplation and description. What are the symbols in the language process? How do they take on meaning? Can we agree on their referents? Can the referents shift behind them, and how? Can the symbols significantly affect the referents? (How true or false is it that sticks and stones will break my bones, but names will never hurt me?) What forces are at work to keep the symbolic process of language relatively stable, though ever changing? What interrelationships are at work between the various symbols? What happens, for instance, to make a series of sounds become a sentence, a series of sentences become a reason for existence?

Perhaps the greatest effort in education needs to be directed toward consideration of language as symbolic process. Half the letters to editors in America, and unfortunately, most of the wars in the modern world, have resulted from failure to recognize some linguistic exercise for what it is—a symbolic exercise, not an absolute truth. I have sat on scores of writing committees, and I know the inaccuracies and approximations and compromises implicit and expressed in the language of whatever document is finally produced as well as the various interpretations that can be given to the words. Yet, once adopted, the words are picked up by flesh-and-blood people and read, and the words become gospel truth or stern criterion or cause at last; so governments rise and fall on misplaced commas, felons go free on a participle, a life is salvaged by a bit of verse, a civilization saved in how great measure by four syllables—"blood, sweat, and tears." Let a high priest groan or a president sigh and crosses can be reared or stock markets dip. A fellow madman and I, faced with a group of two hundred students who were accustomed to a lecture once a week, wondered what would happen if we devised a lecture for them that sounded like meaningful language but was composed entirely of utter nonsense. We wondered how many students would take notes the whole way through. And, of course, I never fail to be struck reactionless at the recognition that a single sound—a *yes* or *no*—in response to a critical combination of other sounds—*Fascist Pigs! Filthy Commies! Revisionist dogs! Forty-second parallel! Let them eat cake! Here I stand! God is Love!*—can begin or end a war, build or wreck a civilization, inspire immortal heroics, and encourage grown men to crush breath from infants who have not yet developed enough as organisms to form the single sound themselves.

There is only one truth available to man caught in this phenomenon of language, an uncomfortable, disarming truth to many: Symbols are negotiable; truth is bedrock and beyond the limits of knowledge and thus of language. This is another way of saying that the only rule to which there can be no exception is that there are exceptions to every rule. Linguistically, we might better ask ourselves in negotiation not whether we are right or wrong but whether or not our sound requires the sacrifice of a life—and if so, is it worth it?

Because language makes it possible for man to tell fellowman an infinite variety of things, transcending both time and place with his words, it is language that gives man his distinctiveness. Neither the opposable thumb nor the higher proportion of brain within the single organism can surpass the magnitude of language as the measure of the grand accomplishment that we call in ourselves *humanity*. The study of language is the study of man, and vice versa. This fact, coupled with the fact of language as symbolic process, makes language the most basic of subjects now offered in the schools. If the total curriculum were reduced to one subject, that subject, label it what you will, is linguistic. By tradition and common consent, a study of humanity has included in most people's minds the study of literature, especially as it is concerned with motivations and forces, drives and affects, events and implications. Yet underlying every utterance in every classroom is the miracle of humanity—man's ability to transcend time and place with his own words. A note to the milkman might survive to eternity, if pencil, paper, and inclination to read last long enough. Thus, the use of language places huge potential responsibility for great things as for frivolous things on every human being.

It is this quality of language—that it allows man to transcend his own time and place as no other animal can—that helps make "progress" possible and without which there would be no history, no science, no belief, no heritage. Any human being, then, who sees himself as no more than a creature of the moment is missing out on most of his own humanity. Heritage is particularly useful as a means toward recognizing the universals of mankind. (Socrates lambasted teenagers as soundly as any contemporary Puritan has.) But heritage is equally effective at centering in on the meaning of a word or the ramification of a concept. (What do *scissors* and *homicide* have in common?) Or in discovering roots of the present in seeds of the past. (You mean Rousseau said that even before A. S. Neill wrote *Summerhill?*) Heritage can help us understand why there are such things as irregular verbs as well as periodic charts, what the historical or socioeconomic difference is between *pork* and *hog*, or how the Gemini space project was named.

Language as the study of man must certainly put students and teachers in touch with the fundamental issue of humanity: whether control of man's life, and indeed his view of the universe, comes from within himself or from without. That basic question manifests in the conflict between authoritarian and descriptive analyst in the great debate over grammar, in the uproar over situational ethics, and in the quandary of many middle-aged Christian church-goers over the fate of the reward-punishment system that depends on belief in a spatial heaven that few people anymore believe exists. Do we try to get each individual to use that set of linguistic conventions for which there is an absolute standard, or do we listen closely to what a number of individuals say, then describe the patterns common among the things they have said? Do we seek the security and stability of a life directed by forces beyond our control, whether medieval-metaphysical forces or Marxist, or do we seek the egoistic, romantic adventure of the inner-directed life? Do we have all one hundred students solve the problem "this way because this is the way that problem is supposed to be solved," or do we hear a hundred separate voices from a hundred sacred individual worlds?

The fundamental question of the human animal echoes through his centuries of self-consciousness. Whatever the label on his class-room door, whatever the title of his course, whatever the thrust of his discipline, severely limited in his humanity is that teacher who does not sometimes reel to the thunder of the echo, who does not strike the challenge again and again into the ears of his students: What is man that thou art mindful of him . . . how infinite in faculty . . . the glory, jest and riddle of the world . . . a tattered coat upon a stick, unless soul clap its hands and sing. . . .[2]

To appreciate language as that which sets man apart from beasts and places him a little lower than the angels, we simply need to learn not to take our everyday uses of language for granted. We are so much blinded by the welter that language has produced and that we call humanity in its boundless array and fragmented variety that we too easily forget that, among the myriad differences among us and our interests and our separate lifeviews and our ways of living, there is language by which hundreds of millions of us communicate, by which we live our lives, write our histories, dream our dreams, bury our dead. There is culture by which we measure our own attitudes and accomplishments. There is humanity by which we set ourselves apart as a race from the rest of creation.

---

[2] These four quotations are, in turn, from *Psalm* 8, William Shakespeare's *Hamlet*, Alexander Pope's *Essay on Man*, and William Butler Yeats' "Sailing to Byzantium," this last reprinted with the permission of M. B. Yeats and The Macmillan Company from *Collected Poems* by William Butler Yeats. Copyright 1928 by The Macmillan Company, renewed 1956 by Georgie Yeats.

I have taken so much time with language here because it is that which binds us together when that which it has produced so often tempts us to draw apart. At the same time, it is that which is our distinction from whatever is nonhuman. As organism, we differ little from other animals—we are, in fact, inferior in bulk to the hippopotamus, in appetite to the earthworm, in speed to the gazelle. As perceiver, we are bettered in hearing by the bat, in touch by the ant, in smell by the bloodhound. In language, nothing is our equal—either in ability to communicate or in capacity for error. Let no one tell me language is not what he is teaching.

And let no one believe that language is not a curse and a blessing simultaneously. There is fault in believing that turning something into a word nails it down forever as a fact. If we were to ignore the phenomenon of change within language, we would be ignoring the unyielding presence of change in life and in humanity itself. There is fault in believing that a word is not private in total meaning to whoever offers or receives the word, fault in believing that a dog is a dog is a dog no matter where the word is used or when or how or by whom. I would like to see us dedicate ourselves to some sort of anti-labellism, for so often we fall into talking in labels and saying nothing. Give me a useful and precise referent for *quality control, society, our students, the public*—all words that freckle conferences, curriculum guides, and calls to educational arms from coast to coast. Or, we exchange labels for labels—"language arts" for "English"; "commercial course" for "non-college preparatory"; "developmental" for "remedial"; "co-curricular" for "after school"—eventually building up precious little verbal distinctions to justify the change or to make ourselves believe there has been a substantial change or to rationalize our protection and conservation of those past investments we choose not to jeopardize. There are as many pitfalls as there is promise in language.

Literalism, which is both necessary to language and a danger to all of us, has led (literally) to human slaughter, whether by martyrdom or by mistaken identity. In order to communicate a belief or an intuitive impulse, for instance, and to test it as an article of faith, one seer or another gropes for language in which to phrase that belief—like "God is love," for instance, or "of the people, by the people, for the people"—however approximate is the language he settles on. All symbolic, quite symbolic, and all quite, quite open to interpretation and misinterpretation, to translation and mistranslation. And before too long, people are killing other people in the name of the "love of God," or global wars break out with all sides claiming righteousness "of the people, by the people, for the people." But the blame so far lies more in the interpretive phenomenon of language than in the practice of extreme literalism. When an exclusive interpretation—whether by one deviate or a mob called "minority" or "majority" or whatever—is compounded in minds, then in actions with some such battle cry as "Root out the evil from our midst!" all sorts of hell can break loose for the poor devil targeted by the particular interpretation of "evil" at hand, for "root" in that figure of speech quite literally means "death," whether by burning or garroting or shooting does not really matter. He might be lucky if someone in the mob recognizes symbolic process for what it is and lets him off with mere deposition or character assassination; at least he will be left inside his skin, literally.

I have taken so much time considering language here because the mere sequence of organic, perceptual man's development of and into humanity has been linguistic and because the basic characteristics of that humanity remain linguistic. Thus, any curriculum, if it is to heighten awareness of human life, of humanity in all its complexity and variety, is fundamentally a linguistic curriculum; or in other terms, it is a humanity-based curriculum, obviously—which is to say, essentially and not so obviously to everybody, that it is language based. On that premise we can now arrive at the first two parts of a tripartite statement of what we are up to in education—or, rather, what we should be up to if our intent remains: (1) to heighten awareness of life, (2) to facilitate exchange of knowledge, perception, and belief so as to sharpen sense of selfhood, if for no social or altruistic reasons, and (3) to aim the individual toward development of wisdom. In short, we are offering the learner experience in *skill, data, concept, theme, attitude,* or *process*—either singly or in combination—on one or more of four levels of human capacity for operation—*organic, perceptual, linguistic, post-linguistic.* We need only agree to what end these experiences are being offered, and quite abruptly I suggest the four ends that I listed earlier as the four basic structures of humanity: the recognition and assimilation by the learner of ever-increasing degrees of or capacity for *unity, diversity, process,* and *substance.* They are all he needs to know (and, I suspect, all there is to know) to lead a full, rewarding life as an integrated individual within a human society. I realize the slipperiness among the various categories I have suggested. I realize that one would be hard put to keep them still, like good little pigeonholes in the post office, or to build neat little impenetrable walls of exclusion or patterns of trespass around or within each one. I want that slipperiness and shiftiness there in our frame of reference, for one reason to keep us dynamic within the context, to forestall smugness and cloture and labelling and a sense of ultimate resolution—to discourage what some participants might choose to accept as final and absolute answer, to discourage certainty that it was indeed a pebble of quartz at the bottom of Frost's well. I want that fluidity within the framework to dramatize the incompleteness, the tentativeness, the ultimate paradoxes that guarantee mystery and curiosity and adventure and movement in human life—to make it something other than rote exercise.

A few words, then, about each of the four basic structures of life, followed by the somewhat whimsical refinement of a linguistic approach to education, the most ideal mystery of all—the poetics of education.

Unity is the abstract phenomenon that allows us to see wholes and entities and order. Without it we could never recognize a dog as distinct from the street it is walking down, nor could we distinguish earth from sky, water from land. There can be unities within a unity: a word has unity, so does a phrase, and a sentence, and a paragraph, and a short story. It can be understood structurally—for instance, as a child gets the "feel" for the rise and fall of an utterance long before he can verbalize (if ever) some definition of a sentence. Unity allows us to recognize a three-legged cat as a freak. Whatever has unity needs nothing to be added to it, and were any part of it taken away, it would no longer be the unit it is. Unity becomes apparent in a sense of direction as well as in purpose. It is essential to the simplest notions as to the most profound and complicated philosophies of life. Unity, when we recognize something in its wholeness, makes it possible for us to bring meaning—to an asterisk or to an era. It allows us to develop systems and bodies of knowledge and standards of judgment. Nonsense is possible because it denies or challenges or violates a sense of unity.

Unity has to do with cohesion, singularity, abstraction, essence. It underlies the belief that we human beings are indeed creatures of a kind that can educate ourselves, that can bring order out of chaos, who are capable of taking aim and bringing focus to experience as it cascades haphazardly in upon us. With no sense of unity we should be as civilized and sophisticated as debris in a gigantic gust of wind.

Every teacher—indeed, every human being—recognizes unity, whether or not he knows he recognizes it. The special responsibility of the teacher is to bring the student to touch unity as a fundamental of human life as often as the occasion to do so arises. That occasion can arise in learning to recognize a word, in learning to call a sentence a sentence, in reading a fable, in looking carefully at a picture, in evaluating a yearbook, in planning a Student Council election campaign, in reading a novel, in writing a research paper, in formulating a philosophy of life, in batting a ball, in turning a piece on a lathe, in building a mathematical construct, in typing a title page.

Diversity is built biologically into human life. No two human beings can bring exactly the same experience to the meaning of any word they hear, just as your left eye or your left ear cannot see or hear the same sensory world exactly as your right eye or your right ear sees or hears it at any one moment. We are forced by nature into diversity, a diversity by which we are enabled to develop perspective, depth, balance, judgement, variety, conflict, and appreciation. Without diversity, life would be as interesting to live as a gelatin blob would be to look at for an eternity or two. Teachers should want their students to recognize diversity in drumbeats as well as in dialects. A composition can come alive by the diversification of the structural patterns and lengths of its components or by the diversification in selecting those components that will be incorporated into whatever composition. Prejudice and blindness can die in an appreciation of the diversity of cultures. Diversity in vocabulary allows greater precision in the use of words and subtler distinctions between one observation or utterance and another. Diversity allows a speaker or writer to recognize differences between the spoken and the written languages, to choose from various conventions of language that will fit various social situations or purposes, to bring flexibility and adaptability into his normal habits. Diversity—through comparison and contrast—has led to theories about the origin and development of man and of physical universe as well as to identification of various periods of history and various characteristics of various styles of operation, of living, of writing, of doing. It leads to evaluation of effectiveness and validity and truth. Diversity makes possible point of view, and that, to paraphrase Frost, makes all the difference.

In seeking order and unity and well-defined direction in a course of study and in putting the course of study into practice, it becomes dangerously simple for a teacher to deny diversity and bring about its death. Diversity keeps us honest and makes everyone of us a bit of a skeptic, for it denies absolutism. It makes dialogue and controversy possible. It guarantees infinity. The tension between unity and diversity nourishes growth. The special responsibility of the educator is to bring himself and his students to recognize, to appreciate, and to welcome diversity and to use it constructively and effectively in learning and in living.

Process and *substance* seem so self-evident and unerring in their definitions that I hardly see need to comment on them. There is being and end and destination and stuff and product, and there is also becoming, means, travel, doing, activity. In my own mind, I think of the two, somehow, as less abstract than unity and diversity, yet I have no trouble coming up with very concrete manifestations of any of the four to offer as examples, and I simultaneously realize that all four are themselves abstractions.

At any rate, as I said earlier, they are as comprehensive and fundamental of and to life and universe and humanity as Earth, Air, Fire, and Water must have seemed to the Greeks, or as Heaven, Earth, and Hell to the simplest among the medieval monastics.

6

The Poetics of Education

Consider, for a starter, the adventure of the blank sheet and hopefully what happens to it: a single phenomenon that lies behind perhaps both the poem and the child in school.

bat

A fine word—quite visual, onomatopoetic in its own way; quite connotative, very substantial in its referent, in the concrete fact behind the word-symbol. A curious sound—playful, with just a touch in it of potential terror or at least intrigue. No? Fascination, then? At any rate, the blankness of the sheet is broken.

That beats about

Those Bs! Beautiful! A bit pugnacious. But still playful. Certainly a bit demanding of some special attention, however tentative or temporary. And where might it beat about?

in caverns

. . . naturally! And, just as appropriately . . .

all alone,

Contriving

Curious turn in that word *contriving*, especially when one has been watching a bat. Blame caverns for the intrusion of contriving, perhaps—and the persistent whimsy of alliteration.

Not to conclude

Come, come. Too much of a good thing. And look what you've done: Contriving, conclude. Ambiguous words if there ever have been ambiguous words! Absolutely two-faced—even three-faced.

against a wall of stone.

All right, now. It rhymes. All right. And puts an end to the cavern, anyhow—and maybe to the bat. But where does that

83

funny business with contrivance and conclusion lead us? To other "senseless" puns that cause a second look at things we take for granted: a heightened awareness, an exchange, an impulse toward wisdom that will make it all make sense? What does it bring us to but . . .

> Mind in the purest play is like some bat
> That beats about in caverns all alone,
> Contriving by a kind of senseless wit
> Not to conclude against a wall of stone.[1]

If Richard Wilbur can ever forgive me for putting his magnificent stanza through such an exercise, I hope he will do it in the spirit of the implied hope for education that lies by analogy in the quatrain —that its participants will indeed contrive by a kind of senseless wit not to conclude against a wall of stone.

What sort of educational experience might we parallel out of this exercise? First, we obviously embarked with the first utterance on an adventure into the unknown, and I have no doubt that, whether Wilbur began with *bat* or with some other word when the poem started to work itself into sound, the stanza represents an adventure into the unknown for both poet and reader. No one knew exactly how it would end (if it would end) or where it would go in the process. Why, then, were we willing to leave the security of the familiar?

In looking for a reason, I could quote Frost again: "Poetry is play on the brink of mystery." Or, again: "A good poem begins in delight and ends in wisdom." Or maybe the simple push of wind against larynx, then of sound against brain took us off the shore— the same sort of impulse that on a larger scale pushes sound into sentence and sentence into reason for existing. And so on. There must be a thousand reasons we could dream up very easily for our willingness to adventure into the unknown, and they would no doubt differ from reader to reader in such variety and to such extent that the reason one reader might offer would be incomprehensible to some other reader among the thousands of willing adventurers.

---

[1] From "Mind," in *Things of This World*, © 1956, by Richard Wilbur. Reprinted by permission of Harcourt Brace Jovanovich, Inc. The entire poem closes this section of the book.

Which leads to another point: the stanza as just received by whoever has read it might at highest level be really a re-creation of the essence of the experience that the author had in originally making the poem. It might even be called an original creation for the fully involved reader for whom the poetry became poetry— original in reading, obviously not in writing. Art is valid only as it is participatory. Wilbur wrote the words, and we credit him properly as poet. The quatrain is no longer only his, however; in fact, we should say that it is now his only as it can be anyone's who participates in it as a work of art by "reading" it. In further fact, to carry the argument to extreme, if he now finds it impossible to participate in the stanza as he reads it, if he can no longer become involved in it, if it is now only so many words or sounds to him, it is not at all poetry for him except in the sense that he is the man who deservedly gets credit for having written it. He, like any other reader, now, could participate in it as poetry or simply receive it as words. Like any other reader, he could be the professor of the humanities, for instance, who is least humanitarian of anyone on campus, or the instructor of religion who can tell you all about God but who has never experienced a moment of authentic worship, or the science teacher who has never proceeded on any project scientifically in his life.

Third, that involvement, if it took place to its fullest capacity, included emotions, compulsions, senses, beliefs, as well as intellect. To put it simply, poetry hits at least all three: heart, head, ear.

Fourth, it is by nature an individual performance, despite the fact that language is a social phenomenon. The reading of the poem as well as its writing is carried out on an individual basis, and, along with the argument for poetry as participatory experience, it can be carried out no other way. In truth, the poem is a different poem for every person who reads it and may even be different each time the same person reads it.

Yet, for all the sanctity and universality these arguments place within the individual reader and for all the relativity and tentativeness that result, therefore, in the social contexts in which both reader and reading exist, the stanza has been created within very real, very arbitrary, very intrinsic, very mechanical limitations. Those limitations are largely *irrelevant* to the poem in that they are not directly one with content and substance or "message," with attitude and stance. Yet, simultaneously, the limitations are quite *relevant* in that they have forced the stanza to become what it is—perhaps even have influenced the content and substance, etc. Such limitations as "edge of paper" and "normal English vocabulary" are not quite as arbitrary as more severe limitations like line length, meter, rhyme scheme, alliteration, and other repetitive conventions in verse, like the framework that becomes the hanger for whatever message there is. The fact remains, in poetry as in school, that the egocentric thrust of individuality works within a framework—however arbitrary—that more often than not seems a limitation, even a barrier. If poetry results from the struggle, can the individual as creatively survive the institution—more than survive, can it creatively *result* from the grappling that seems inevitable between the two taken at their extremes? More fundamentally, could the individual recognize himself as an individual if there were no anti-individual against which to develop a thrust?

Finally, in light of most of the first five parallels here, it becomes obvious that the stanza—like any other poetry—cannot be paraphrased. It has no identical twin. If its "meaning" is wrapped up with emotions and momentary experience and individual universes, we can hardly expect it to be reproducible.

More of all these matters and concerns and ideas as we proceed, but for now, maybe the moral for education is dramatized—quite without the poet's intent, I am sure—by Donald Hall's poem:

THE SLEEPING GIANT[2]

(A Hill, so Named, in Hamden, Connecticut)

The whole day long, under the walking sun
That poised an eye on me from its high floor,
Holding my toy beside the clapboard house
I looked for him, the summer I was four.

I was afraid the waking arm would break
From the loose earth and rub against his eyes
A fist of trees, and the whole country tremble
In the exultant labor of his rise;

---

[2] From *The Alligator Bride: Poems New and Selected* by Donald Hall. Copyright © 1955 by Donald Hall. Originally appeared in *The New Yorker* and reprinted by permission of Harper & Row, Publishers.

Then he with giant steps in the small street
Would stagger, cutting off the sky, to seize
The roofs from house and home because we had
Covered his shape with dirt and planted trees;

And then kneel down and rip with fingernails
A trench to pour the enemy Atlantic
Into our basin, and the water rush,
With the streets full and all the voices frantic.

That was the summer I expected him.
Later the high and watchful sun instead
Walked low behind the house, and school began,
And winter pulled a sheet over his head.

". . . and school began,/And winter pulled a sheet over his head." The giant killed so painlessly, yes, but with his death, a second quiet demise, another bloodless acquiescence, another putting away of "childish things," another September, another opening of school —perhaps concomitant with a poignant closing of things more precious in life, even sleeping giants who keep us quite alive.

The "poetics of education"—how valid is the notion? How far can we extend the metaphor? How valuable is the analogy? If language is the common characteristic of mankind, if it is that which distinguishes humanity from nonhumanity, if it is the singular phenomenon or process which has made "civilization" possible for man, which allows us to bring order out of chaos, certainly poetry—the quintessence of language—offers a subject ripe for contemplation and exploration of all our notions: of humanity, civilization, order, life, education. If you find Unity, Diversity, Process, and Substance epitomized anywhere, it is in poetry. Even the coldest data scholar, the complete nonparticipant, recognizes a number of obvious basic processes at work in a poem: creation and re-creation, stimulus and response, meter and ego-centric thrust, the symbolic process of metaphor. There is substance in whatever has been observed and labelled in the content or statement or "stuff" that the words and phrases of the poem represent or suggest. A poem's beginning-middle-endness, if nothing else, gives it a unity, and diversity is evident in its tension between mechanics and cry, between system and soul, between the discipline that marks it as verse and regularity and the outrage or elation or despair that lifts it into poetry and mystery. If it is validly a creative experience, the poem has grown ultimately from the organic foundation of listening to one's own blood run, through checking one's own perceptions, into language that says something about life. By analogy, if language is the basis of humanity and poetry is the quintessence of language and if education is to be the quintessence of human life, poetics—the study of how poetry works—should offer us certain instruction in how education at an ideal level might work.

I consider the adventure of the blank sheet and hopefully what happens to it, and a beautiful fiction comes to mind—a fiction incarnate every fall in the freshly scrubbed, wide-eyed innocence of six-year-olds gathering from scattered backyards and sidewalks and swimming pools, gathering in the blacktopped play area or on the bus loading platform or in front of the huge doors or around the stone steps of the main entrance to the school building. Blank sheets, we see in them (perhaps our first mistake as schoolmen) hope for a thousand new creations. What will institutionalized education offer them, make of them? Everyone a potential poem? Every bright-eyed individual guaranteed poetic experience as it moves toward inevitable confrontation with the institution it is entering for the first inescapable time?

I think of the compulsion and need that so many poets have apparently felt for their pouring themselves out on paper or at least for their throwing themselves into the arbitrary rigor and irrational discipline that poetry requires, and I wonder how close the parallel with what educators have so glibly and euphemistically been kicking around as "felt need" in their students. I think of the struggle and process and labor and love that such drive initiates and maintains in the poet, and I wonder how it is that schools might encourage similar struggle and process and labor and love as the natural lifeblood of the students who might come to those schools with wellsprings of motivation and need similar to the poet's in depth and intensity. Or, might I better draw parallel between poet and what the teacher might be—finding his own best therapy in offering the experience that the student might re-create, in turn, as his own learning, his own poetry?

Connotation, the art of suggestion, which poetry uses as no other kind of language does, brings to my mind the notion that no one *teaches* another person anything—that the most effective teachers simply make it conducive for the student to learn. The hypnotist, I have been told, hypnotizes no one; he simply makes the bed through suggestion on which the "hypnotized" puts himself into trance. There is no teaching; there is only learning. And suddenly the foolish idea that there can be only "one right answer" fades into perspective and out of mind. That kids re-create when learning rather than merely receive reminds me that their learning will be facilitated in direct proportion to their emotional and psychic and sensory involvement as well as their intellectual awareness. It is the art of suggestion, of connotation, not of direct statement, that encourages such involvement, that makes the bed on which the student can lie down if he is ready for it.

I think of the bane that didacticism is for the purest imagist admirer of poetry, and it parallels itself for me with the death through predictability that has stricken so many lessons and teachers and programs and books. Consistency and dependability—yes. It would be rather weird not to know if the school building would be standing on its usual site from morning to morning or that Miss Carpenter is the teacher who willingly listens to woes when no one else seems to want to. But complete predictability—deadly boring. What happens to learning as adventure into unknown? Must the same faces behind the same desks be faced in exactly the same order, saying completely predictable things in completely predictable order, day after day after day? Watch the neighborhood kids play "school"—one day after school, when they think no one (that is, no adult) is watching. See how soon the predictable, stereotyped role is assumed by the one who plays "teacher." Folded arms, lack of smile when order is desired, bossiness, and teaching, teaching, teaching—mouthing the platitudes and clichés and irrelevancies that everyone who is going to know already knows either through common sense or independent discovery or earlier learning. Calling for upraised hands and tightly closed lips (at the same time the real teacher tells herself and others that she wants spontaniety and open involvement).

When I watch words turn into metaphor and metaphor into passion and strength and beauty and profundity—into *mystery* at

the hands of our best poets—I wonder how it is that the stuff of
life so often becomes drudgery when it gets turned into curriculum
and instruction. Is there some unbridgeable difference between the
life that feeds poetry and the life that feeds schooling? How can
there be? Why should there be? Why must education become the
sterile seeking for accepted and previously approved answers when
Yeats' magnificent "Leda" so concisely moves the reader from
simple sound through pulsing sensuality into quest after the sources
and transfer and movement and uses of knowledge and power,
into quest after the ways of men and of gods?

LEDA AND THE SWAN[3]

A sudden blow: the great wings beating still
Above the staggering girl, her thighs caressed
By the dark webs, her nape caught in his bill,
He holds her helpless breast upon his breast.

How can those terrified vague fingers push
The feathered glory from her loosening thighs?
And how can body, laid in that white rush,
But feel the strange heart beating where it lies?

A shudder in the loins engenders there
The broken wall, the burning roof and tower
And Agamemnon dead.
                            Being so caught up,
So mastered by the brute blood of the air,
Did she put on his knowledge with his power
Before the indifferent beak could let her drop?

William Butler Yeats

The myth of Zeus' seduction of Leda while he is disguised as a
beautiful swan, the ensuing birth of Helen, whose beauty inspires
the cataclysmic Trojan War and the deaths of so many great men,
including Agamemnon. From the same story source, of what would
the typical classroom lesson be built: dates of the war, list of major
battles, sketchy map of the area, short biographies of a few of the

---

[3] Reprinted with the permission of M. B. Yeats and The Macmillan Company
from *Collected Poems* by William Butler Yeats. Copyright 1928 by The Macmillan
Company, renewed 1956 by Georgie Yeats.

leaders, some silly fairytale synopsis of the myth, four or five very boring lectures, and a couple of extra-credit projects culled out of the handiest encyclopedia. The indifference of students would be ensured before the topic opened simply by the shortsighted approach we would give it—an indifference extremely alien to the indifference of Zeus' cynicism and spent lust. Of course, one would need handle the story with care in the classroom, at any rate. No mention of rape or mayhem or guile in the typical classroom. They are too much part of the world (whether we like it or not).

One short digression is too pertinent and priceless for me to fight at this point. I have long chuckled that in one of the most popular anthologies in use in high school literature courses, the title of Robert Herrick's poem "To the Virgins, to Make Use of Time" has been changed to "Counsel to Girls." Ah, Robert, if only we could resurrect your seventeenth-century Anglican clerical presence to have at these bounders! The anthology goes unnamed by me. Look it up yourself, if you're curious over such tidbits.

Metaphor and mystery, curriculum and instruction? Education remains an adventure into the unknown only for the student, and then into an unknown that has previously been explored and certified as "worth the effort" by those teachers and seers of society and tradition who have been there before—whether or not as original explorers of virgin territory we shall not ask. Is it an impossible hope that someday the institution—the practice and formal procedures of education itself—will share with its students an authentic adventure into the unknown, an adventure that would find the institution risking as much as it expects the student to risk? As it now stands, only the student can fail, as far as the official record is concerned. If education is more often to become "play on the brink of mystery," the school is somehow going to have to learn playfulness to a level that most kids have achieved well before they have entered school. Playfulness requires an element of risk. How an institution might develop such a human characteristic is a question worth tossing around. For a starter, I do not think it develops playfulness, for instance, by determining ahead of time an unalterable calendar and a comprehensive, prescriptive course of study, then compounding such rigidity with unquestioned procedures of student pigeonholing and skeleton techniques of certification of achievement according to simple perseverence and acquiescence. (As one former colleague phrased it when he was asked what it really took to earn his master's degree: "Plenty of money and a good strong bottom!") Can we, rather, give priority to placing our students so they will more often touch the boundless universe and to letting them connect through time with some feeling for infinity? Can we at least begin to question traditional categories—whether of scheduling, or placement, or subject matter, or instructional techniques, or whatever?

I recognize the poem as performance in words—with all the connotations the word *performance* holds for practice and discipline and serendipity and circumstance and the rest. Then, I wonder that we do not more openly and extensively recognize that both teaching and learning can be performing arts, too—especially teaching. Strange that we do not go up to a great comedian and say, "Sorry I missed your act. Do you have a book I can read to make up for it?" Or, that we do not go up to a psychotherapist and say, "Too bad that I missed my appointment with you today. May I borrow your notes to fill the gap?" Or, that we do not skip the show and simply mingle with the crowd after it has left the theater, hoping that we can somehow share, secondhand, the catharsis it has undergone during the dramatic performance inside the theater, if the drama has evoked catharsis. Yet, by our attitudes and actions, many of us regularly make such statements to a special class of performers—the best classroom teachers in our schools. If education is at all worthwhile and if there is a need in it for a kind of person known as "teacher," then we must realize that the best teachers are excellent performers in the best sense of the word.

There is no substitute or "makeup" for a good learning experience developed and guided by a good teacher. No book in the world, no set of notes, no tape recording can hope to simulate or record in all its subtlety, nuance, emotion, and personal involvement that unique human event known as a successful moment of learning. In the last analysis, books, lesson plans, notes, tests, and audio-visual techniques are not what is unique about a successful teacher. His performance—maybe "charisma" gets close—is to a great extent what sets the good teacher apart from the average or poor one. That performance might take place in front of three hundred students, or with only one. Asking such a teacher for a reading assignment that will make up for the classroom session that someone has missed is exactly like asking Marcel Marceau for a book that will do the same thing for you that his pantomime might have done had you sat in the theater and witnessed it. That is why the good teacher can probably teach well no matter what textbook or equipment is or is not allotted to him.

The point here is not to disparage textbooks, lesson plans, audio-visual devices, demonstration equipment, and the like. A boy could hardly learn to operate a lathe if there were no lathe in the school shop. Likewise, the teacher without a clear sense of direction might confuse more students than he guides. But the point is that a good teacher is certainly not the sum of textbooks, lesson plans, audio-visual devices, equipment, and the like that he uses in his course. Much of the magic that identifies teaching or learning at its best is spontaneous, serendipitous, irretrievable. The greatest actor in the world cannot guarantee that his every moment on stage will represent a high in dramatic art. But let such a high moment be attained—no matter how rare or brief the moment—and, like a poetic experience, it can never be replaced or recaptured. So it is with the best moments for learning in the classroom. "For him we batter our hands/Who has won for once over the world's weight."

JUGGLER[4]

A ball will bounce, but less and less. It's not
A light-hearted thing, resents its own resilience.
Falling is what it loves, and the earth falls
So in our hearts from brilliance,
Settles and is forgot.
It takes a sky-blue juggler with five red balls

To shake our gravity up. Whee, in the air
The balls roll around, wheel on his wheeling hands,
Learning the ways of lightness, alter to spheres
Grazing his finger ends,
Cling to their courses there,
Swinging a small heaven about his ears.

[4] Copyright, 1949, by Richard Wilbur. Reprinted from his volume, *Ceremony and Other Poems* by permission of Harcourt Brace Jovanovich, Inc. First published in *The New Yorker*.

But a heaven is easier made of nothing at all
Than the earth regained, and still and sole within
The spin of worlds, with a gesture sure and noble
He reels that heaven in,
Landing it ball by ball,
And trades it all for a broom, a plate, a table.

Oh, on his toe the table is turning, the broom's
Balancing up on his nose, and the plate whirls
On the tip of the broom! Damn, what a show, we cry:
The boys stamp, and the girls
Shriek, and the drum booms
And all comes down, and he bows and says goodbye.

If the juggler is tired now, if the broom stands
In the dust again, if the table starts to drop
Through the daily dark again, and though the plate
Lies flat on the table top,
For him we batter our hands
Who has won for once over the world's weight.

Richard Wilbur

More often than to any of these other thoughts, I turn to the
movement and interplay, in poetry, back and forth among meter,
mechanics, counterpoint, and cry—that progression or mutual need
or subtle merging and balance between polarized *structure* (the
extrinsic, the arbitrary, the mechanical) and *egocentric thrust* (the
internal, the personal, the sacred, the compulsive toward selfhood
and individuality). It shows up when I consider the difference
between poetry, which includes all elements named in our discussion here, and verse, which simply uses the arbitrary framework of
poetry as an attention-getter for a prosy statement, and when I
think of parallel differences within the typical school between humanity or soul and all the impersonal elements that so often seem
to overwhelm until such personal concern lapses into silent obliv-
ion. We cannot listen to Alice's worries about the pending collapse
of her family because there is a class to be met, a schedule to be
kept. Too bad that Jim is ready for Boolean algebra; most of the
other kids in the class are somewhere in the elementaries, and we
cannot take time for Jim, nor cut him loose with no one looking
over him, because of legal liability and distrust of the implications
such granting of independence and responsibility would hold for

the demands of other students similarly overwhelmed by the system.

Generalized, I suppose this concern has to do mostly with a seeking for a point of balance between individual and institution, for no one wants to be exactly like everyone else. Mediocrity is madness; anonymity nothingness. Yet no one can live in a vacuum of his own individualistic making, for man is at least biologically a social being, and his language evidence that humanity requires non-insularity of its members. Non-insularity requires—almost presumes —system.

It is curious enough to me that some of the unique, most moving, most personal statements in our language have been made through poetic form of one kind or another, with all the artificial limitations such form can impose. It is absolutely miraculous, paradoxical, that of those most personal, most moving, unique poetic statements, many have been worked out within highly artificial, extremely sophisticated conventions of form—among them, the sonnet, terza rima, heroic couplet, and above all the mathematical and mosaic-like sestina. My fascination with this phenomenon of struggle is no less compelling when I hear poets confess that the best poetry results often from the mutual creation that the form and the poet work out together—that neither poet is exclusively responsible, nor is form, that whatever is truly poetic and creative in the result is a joint effort, a delicate compromise between the egocentric thrust of the poet's impulses and intent and the limitations of language and rhyme and meter and stanza form and the rest. Dave Brubeck's famous jazz recording of *Take Five* has always struck me as the perfect example in music of the same phenomenon of happy balance in this conflict between statement and framework for statement.

When I realize the two directions in which tipping that balance can go, my fascination turns almost to fixation, then collapses in utter frustration at trying to predict or engineer or somehow institutionalize the fragile entente. How often in school as in poetry the form seems so demanding that personal impulse and intent capitulate or are inundated in the confrontation: conventional limitations in class size, duration and frequency of periods, semester lengths, number of years sustained, number of credits accumulated, number of pages "covered," and the like. Or, the form is easily mastered, the conventional framework easily achieved, but with no thrust, no message, no substance worth the effort. One merely survives twelve years in an institution—or sixteen years, or twenty —and one thinks one is therefore educated. I recall a proud teacher bringing me a "sonnet" that one of her high school seniors had produced in 1960. The exact year is so clear in my mind because of the appalling substance of the verse. Nixon and John Kennedy were running for the Presidency that year, and the girl had spent her first quatrain, in perfect rhyme and proper iambic pentameter, extolling the virtues of Richard M. Nixon, the second quatrain in doing the same for John F. Kennedy (equal time), the third quatrain assuring us that either man (being American, I suppose) would make an excellent President, and the conclusive couplet urging us to "get out the vote." If only the inscription had been tiny enough or a metal disc large enough, the girl would have had a remarkable campaign button. But she hardly had a sonnet, whether or not the piece ended up looking like fourteen lines of iambic pentameter rhymed according to the Elizabethan pattern and structured according to one sonnet convention. (No pun intended on convention.)

This delicate balance between individual and institution, between personal impulse and impersonal form takes me always to another insistence of Frost's: that English poetry results from the tension in a line between basic meter and the rhythms of normal speech. But, ah! To achieve that tension—to prevent Shelley's "The lone and level sands stretch far away" from lapsing into some sixth grader's "Empty desert stretching/As far as eye (pun) can see." So often we lose sight of the reasons for the rules in the first place, for the function of system and framework, and thus, whether in misguided benevolence or unconscious habit, we so often kill the creature we so much treasure.

DEATH OF A BIRD[5]

A few days after.
After we had put him into the letterbox
And made a home for him
From this

---

[5] Copyright © 1958 by Jon Silkin. Reprinted from *Poems New and Selected*, by Jon Silkin, by permission of Wesleyan University Press.

Outrageous cage of wire
Long and shallow where the sunlight fell
Through the air onto him;
After

He had been fed for
Three days, suddenly in the late morning
He was dead, without any
Pretence.

He did not say goodbye
He did not say thank you. But he died
Lying flat on the rigid
Wires

Of his cage, his gold
Beak shut tight, which once in hunger
Had opened enormously like
A large

Trap, and closed again
Swallowing quickly what had been given him.
How can I say I am sorry
He died.

Seeing him lie there
Friendly with death I was angry he had gone
Without pretext or warning,
Without

A suggestion first he should
Go, since we had fed him and made him safe
And bade him hop over our
Hands. We

Asked him only that
He should desire life. He had become
Of us, a black friend with a
Gold mouth

Shrilly singing through
The heat. The labour of the black bird! I
Cannot understand why
He is dead.

I bury him familiarly
His heritage is a small brown garden.
Something is added to the everlasting earth;
From my mind a space is taken away.

Jon Silkin

There is little question that form and framework and boundary are necessary—if not for the sake of control, then in the name of economy and efficiency. It is simply wasteful for everyone to go his own way and chaotic if no one is even able to recognize that it is indeed a way that he is himself going, all alone or not. Simply opening up one's larynx and letting sound gargle out does not make a poem—or even make sense, usually. Yet, if the stamp of individuality is never allowed to develop within the individual, he too has lost meaning. Somehow, we must devise an educational scheme through which men may move and by which they will thus be enabled to cast it off sooner or later as a no-longer-necessary shell.

SAND DUNES[6]

Sea waves are green and wet,
But up from where they die
Rise others vaster yet,
And those are brown and dry.

They are the sea made land
To come at the fisher town
And bury in solid sand
The men she could not drown.

She may know cove and cape,
But she does not know mankind
If by any change of shape
She hopes to cut off mind.

Men left her a ship to sink:
They can leave her a hut as well;

And be but more free to think
For the one more cast-off shell.

Robert Frost

Somehow, the unerring mission of formal schooling must become to develop men who are capable of being "but more free to think/For. the one more cast-off shell," if it is not doing so in sufficient number and with sufficient surety now. In pursuit of that mission, it seems clear that a structure must be developed that will enable the school itself to begin early to recognize that ultimate freedom and the responsibility to and of individual human beings that such freedom requires.

Of the several schemes now popular in scheduling and organizing American schools, I suppose the familiar lockstep pattern stands at one extreme—the one least conducive to freedom and most suspicious of individual responsibility, except to conformity. Graphically, it looks like a simple, unimaginative, cross-line grid:

					Pupils
					Classes
					Teachers
					Time
					Space
					Subjects

While many of those who work with the pattern and defend it recognize all its shortcomings, the shortcomings exist all the same —with oftentimes stifling predictability and stricture. Essentially, no matter how hard we try to manipulate the grid or to maneuver within it, it remains a simple, cross-line grid, and pupils get fed into it and file out of it treated relatively the same one to another— as do teachers, blocks of time, instructional groupings, assignments of space and facility, and various subject disciplines, topics, activities, or resources.

At the other extreme, the completely open plan—rarely if ever practiced, though often claimed—moves so far toward freedom that I for one fear for the absence of system, not so much because of the sacrifice of institutional control over participants, but more so because of the potential loss of efficiency and economy, because of the almost unlimited potential for waste motion, for complete lack of direction:

I recognize that my fears can be allayed with proper administration and staffing and resource and all the rest, but when I ask advocates of the open "system" to spell out the means of such "proper administration," more often than not it turns out that they have retained certain controls through "Teachers" or "Space" or in "Subjects" or in some other way, and the "openness" is more delusion than design or practice.

Or, they end up describing to me a third kind of scheme—not really open at all, though similarly pointed toward greater individualization of instruction than the block pattern usually allows. They describe something that finds its most systematic manifestation in the best "flexible" or "modular" or "variable" school structures in the country. While the number of different patterns or modifications available within such structures is astronomical, especially with the aid of a computer, the essential distinction of flexible or modular from block structure and from open structure might graphically look something like this:

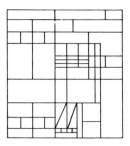

If institutions must have boundaries, if schools must have schedules and organizational schemes, I suppose this third kind, the "flexible" or "modular" one, is the best one now in popular use—best in that it comes closest to a neat balance between individual and institution. At least it offers variety that the block structure does not, and where it works well, there is plenty of freedom and responsibility for the participant, too. It is still, however, strongly weighted toward institution—much more strongly in that direction than towards the individual.

I have been told many times that my quest for an institution that can reflect human qualities—for a form that can be as variegated and adaptable as a human's frame of reference, for instance, or for a mechanism that can encourage diversity and be sensitive to feelings—that such a quest is at last doomed to frustration. There is a strict dichotomy, I am advised, between individual human beings and the institutions that such humans develop and maintain. Individuals will always be human beings, whether or not they like it, and institutions will always be at last utterly non-human, although *human* and *nonhuman* are not usually the terms used in the argument. Rather, there are *personal* institutions and *impersonal* ones, I am always reminded, and the differences between them lie in the qualities of the various *persons* who make them up—in their different points of view, in their separate definitions of institution, in the varying uses they make of those institutions, and the like.

I hear the advice, but my quest continues. I simply am not convinced that responsive as well as responsible educational organization cannot be developed. It strikes me that in such organization lies the major breakthrough that will allow man to enter more fully and comfortably into the new phase of human evolution that technology is now making possible. I am very much in hopes that like Wilbur's bat, with which we began this section of inquiry, we might yet come up with some "very happiest intellection" that will make of the entire establishment a new institution for a new kind of education.

MIND[7]

Mind in the purest play is like some bat
That beats about in caverns all alone,
Contriving by a kind of senseless wit
Not to conclude against a wall of stone.

It has no need to falter or explore;
Darkly it knows what obstacles are there,

_____

[7] From *Things of This World*.

And so may weave and flutter, dip and soar
In perfect courses through the blackest air.

And has this simile a like perfection?
The mind is like a bat. Precisely. Save
That in the very happiest intellection
A graceful error may correct the cave.

Richard Wilbur

Robert Frost had a good bit to say about poetry: "A good poem begins in delight and ends in wisdom." "Poetry is play on the brink of mystery." "Poetry is an attempt to bring order out of chaos." To all of these, I would add, "So it should be with education."

Frost wrote, ". . . school and poetry come so near being one thing."[8] To that, I would add, obviously, *amen.* My immediate question concerns how the nearness can be contracted. How close can we bring educational structure to poetic ideal? Can we come up with some very happiest intellection that may correct the cave we beat about while practicing school?

------

[8] From "Maturity No Object," by Robert Frost, an introduction to *The New Poets of England and America,* ed. by Donald Hall, Robert Pack, and Louis Simpson, copyright © 1957 by the World Publishing Company. Other prose or conversational quotations from Frost used throughout my book I heard from Frost himself at various times from 1957 through 1962 when I was a student and he patriarchal visitor at the Bread Loaf School of English, which he helped found at Middlebury College, Middlebury, Vermont.

7

Compromise—One Practical Alternative

"Let them pile the bricks in on me, but let me build with them for myself."[1]

One day my daughter came home from school with five sentences on a paper.

> Do you want me?
> Will you help me.
> Where is my ball?
> Are the boys here?
> Can you run fast?

Her teacher had marked the second sentence wrong (and I probably would have done the same thing in her position) because the girl had not followed it with a question mark, and the teacher added some such note as "Please help her to recognize a question." Now, I suspect, laying aside prejudice for my own child, that the girl recognized the fact, even though she could not verbalize it, that socially the sentence "Will you help me?" does not—at least in our home—usually call forth the same kind of basically verbal response that the other four questions can be expected to call forth. I also suspect that she recognized the utterance "Will you help me?" as what we at our home would consider a polite command or perhaps a statement of need or a request—not really a question to which an answer is unknown at the moment of utterance. That subtle distinction might easily be jeopardized or lost in the child by a teacher's insistence on a question mark for some wrong or oversimplified reason—with such an explanation, for in-

---

[1] A remark a large group of us heard Frost make at the Bread Loaf School of English, Middlebury, Vermont, one summer evening in the late fifties or early sixties.

stance, as "Put a question mark there because a question is a question and all questions must be followed by question marks."

So much for some of the language lesson that can be drawn from the experience. Now for a point or two in our quest for an alternative to what we now generally have in the typical practice of education. Here was an individual—Daughter—being served by an institution—school. Unfortunately—and there is little that Teacher could have done differently, given the present stone wall structure of that cave or institution she represents—Teacher misread the blank sheet, most likely, for the sheet was not honest-to-goodness blank when it came under her direction. How was Teacher to know, how could she ever know, the language habits and sound patterns and social customs in practice in Daughter's home ever since the day Daughter was born—six and a half years of history earlier? (What had gone on in American political history during the same period of time? John F. Kennedy's election, the Cuban missile crisis, the Berlin Wall, Kennedy's assassination, early fantastic space flights by man, Johnson's landslide over Goldwater, and the Beatle's triumphant conquest of the United States.) Furthermore, Teacher met Daughter in a roomful of thirty, each Son and Daughter of them bringing with him a separate and unique private variety and level of sophistication and experience in matters linguistic. Little wonder that the impersonal Institution—both that institution known as "classroom" and that institution known as "question marks"—little wonder that it prevailed over personal Individual. Perhaps a small demise, this one, but still one more point against the human individual, and scored by the educational institution that has been built intentionally and sincerely in her behalf. That way poems are not made; they are turned into alphabetical lists of otherwise disconnected words.

Perhaps we should recognize once again that schooling is not education and that education is not synonymous with learning. *Learning* has to do with development, with the addition of some piece of knowledge or some aptitude to a person's total ability, with a change of behavior, or with the modification of a lifestyle or lifeview. It can hardly help but happen from birth to death, with or without educational institution. Learning can be an unselfconscious phenomenon. That is, the learner need not be aware that he is learning, nor is the process necessarily recognized nor the phenomenon organized specifically as a "learning experience."

Maybe Daughter had learned, without school experience, how "Will you help me?" in the context of her particular family differed from "Do you want me?" *Education* is guided learning, guided usually though not necessarily through interaction of the learner with one or more other persons, either directly, as in a personal conference or in a discussion group, or indirectly, as through film or recording or textbook. The business of education is learning—conscious learning, though not always overt learning, learning with the added dimension that during his education, the learner is aware that he is learning, or supposed to be. *Schooling* is primarily institutional in character and refers more to the mechanics, or structure, by which education is most often supposed to be facilitated. Our present system of certification—high school diplomas, awarding of degrees, and the like—is a rather accurate measure of *schooling* but a thickly foggy method of communicating *educational* experience and a point-zero one of indicating level or kind or amount of *learning* achieved. If schooling is to provide in fact more of what it is commonly and by tradition thought to be up to and if it is to do so economically and efficiently, it needs to be rather thoroughly redesigned.

It is like spitting into the rain to say that the problems involved are complex indeed. It is madness to believe that some systematic solution can be proffered that will harness the wild gesticulations and satisfy a bit of the insistent hunger that have ranged adolescently over this inquiry, this quest. Yet, maturity—of quest or of institution—lies always just ahead like a mustang yearning to be tamed at last, and I might—only might—have both harness and hay in hand.

What about the problem of the eternal triangle—person, institution, idea? Can the three at last be separated from each other for clearer consideration while we dream our dream? Can the institution be separated from the man, and the man from the idea, so that idea might at last be institutionalized with or without the presence of the man? Can we talk about doing away with Miss Jones' classroom without threatening to do away with Miss Jones? Can we somehow individualize instruction without compromising too hard with the individuals being instructed?

Can we reestablish responsibility as a two-way thrust between Institution and Individual? Can we recognize that responsibility on the part of learner is not a mere responsibility to bow down to the standards and control of the unchallenged institution? Can we also recognize that a mature individual is responsible to more than self, that without his interaction with institution, the economy and efficiency available to him through institution are jeopardized and finally destroyed?

"The trouble with school systems," said a college freshman in an informal seminar, "is that they are built on distrust of students, and ninety-five per cent of us are trustworthy." Can we build an institution that will be responsible in serving its students as its students will be responsible in maintaining the institution? Can we build an institution that will take equal risk with its students, that will set itself as vulnerable to failure and defeat as all students are in most present institutions of education?

Can we agree that the heaviest responsibility a person can assume is the responsibility for living his life as he lives it, in his own name, and as a member of society, and can we design an institution that will grant the individual freedom to develop and practice that responsibility?

Can we recognize that quality education is not necessarily synonymous with an instructor's forcing three hundred separate questions on his students during a final examination in high school biology, that he did not "really earn his pay" and "prove his worth as a teacher" just because he made every kid in the class liable to sweat and tedium and anxiety and eventual fatigue?

I am ready to act on the belief that an individual can be as pluralistic as a society can be, that he therefore can legitimately seek an assortment of educational experiences that might look like a hodge-podge to someone else, and that he therefore can legitimately want to "change his course of study" far more often than once a year—or than once in four years, or eight, or twelve, as is now the case in many school careers in which eighth or ninth graders are asked to choose, essentially, between "college prep" or "non-college prep." I am certain that he is a unique combination of a far greater diversity of unities and partial unities and processes and faltering processes than even he himself is capable of verbalizing and that every moment finds him to be a different combination than he was the moment before. For all the labor, for all the sustained attention, for the cohesion it requires, a book is no more synonym for its author than a poem is for its poet, or a statement for its speaker, or a birdhouse for its builder.

Recognizing such pluralism and diversity and flux in every person as in society and language and life itself, I am certain that *continuity of course presentation* and *coverage of subject matter* are ideals that exist most strongly—perhaps solely—in the mindsets and consciences of the teachers who see them. We admit that fact every time we complain in June that the kids do not remember what we "taught" them in September. We encourage such failure to see continuity and coverage when we as history teachers act as if every kid's schedule reads something like ours: "history" pretty much in every slot, day in and day out. We tend to forget that theirs reads "history, then geography, then spelling, then music, then . . . ," and all punctuated by the vibrancy and giddiness of being young and growing. Still wonder why they seem so "slow" at picking up threads from yesterday's lesson when their school schedules and, a thousand times more so, the fabrics of life unravel so variously and inevitably different from person to person?

I will now entertain—indeed, welcome—for its own sake and in its own size and shape, any learning experience, any instructional activity, any notion that comes along for the curriculum. We have lost or debilitated too many valuable moments or exchanges or ideas simply because they have come in packages either too short or too shallow or too simple to turn into one-semester courses. Or else we have stretched them beyond the breaking point to make them fit. I remember the liberating new dimensions that became available to writers and performers of popular music when technology provided long-playing discs and then tape recordings, both of which made the earlier three-minute recording an unnecessary stricture. Suddenly, a nine and a half minute composition was allowed nine and a half minutes on the recording, and one selection on a favorite album of mine consumes all of ten seconds. Our Procrustean schools, though, seem hard put to envision much outside of fifty-minute periods, two or three or five times a week (depending on the level of schooling involved) in six- or nine- or twelve- or sixteen-week chunks, etc. (The latest "way-out experiment" in many colleges is to give a midyear one- or two- or four-week independent project period to the student for potential credit!) Furthermore, if there is no textbook for the course, the value of the experience and the intentions—yea, the morality—of the instructor are immediately suspect. I am tempted to turn the question around and ask more legitimately, if there is a good well-chosen textbook for the course and the students can read, why the course requires a teacher?

I am ready to seek educational unity not in "my course," but in the student's life—as much as possible in the total school structure, in the total curriculum, in the educational experience as it develops within him or comes to him or as he shapes it for himself. I see no categories or departments that are not of my own sight or making, and I see none for the student that are not of his own vision or making or unforced acceptance. I do not want to snuff out the Einstein or Galileo or William Blake in any man, no matter how small the chances any of them might exist in him, nor to whatever insignificant measure. In truth, I believe there is that primitive element in each man that creates his universe for him. Some men simply delegate the gift to others—or have it delegated before they are aware of what is happening.

Those of us who have disliked or distrusted economy and efficiency have probably done so because their application has seemed so often to frustrate individuality and stifle creativity, to repress wildness and discourage genius. If, however, the principles of economy and efficiency can be applied toward increasing the chances for individuality to mature, toward expanding the arenas in which genius can flourish, then we would be foolish to ignore them. I am ready to propose an institution built solely on the idea that the main reason for grouping, for putting two or more individuals together in a common experience, for establishing an institution, is not to control or police but to serve those individuals more economically and efficiently than can be done if they were to remain exclusively separate from each other.

We are close to the day—indeed if our financial and social priorities were different, we would have arrived at the day—when most of the goals of a purely data curriculum might more economically and efficiently be met by technological means, by indirect human contact, by something other than "teachers teaching" in front of classes. We have long passed that day when subject matter specialists in every field of knowledge are available to the thousands of schools in America in sufficient quantity and quality to service the demands of tens of millions of widely varying individual students. Impossible expectation! And probably has been for several centuries now. I pass new schools in construction, open-mouthed at the mountains of brick and steel and concrete going into them. I grow a bit sad at the thought of the archaic teaching practices and unquestioned academic programs and approaches they will house and harden into physical institution as well as emotional and traditional institutions. Prenatal obsolescence! Then, I yearn for just half the billions in bond issues and cash reserves and investment portfolios and endowments and rising tuitions that are being poured into such effort to modify the academic skyline with yet another stack of bricks and steel and concrete that will be called an "improvement in education." What we might do with minds instead of monuments if we had all that money at our hands! If some of our goals in education can be met more economically and efficiently through technology, let us meet them that way. Then we can let man more consistently be about what is distinctively his to be about. I do not learn sonnets and psycholinguistics so I can sharpen pencils with my teeth.

I am certainly prepared to plunge schooling into the business of providing education—that is, of facilitating learning by economy and efficiency—for everyone, from rattle in hand to rattle in heart. We are all centuries overdue in devising a system of credentialling that reflects the person and his ability rather than the meaningless steps of whatever anonymous—sometimes gutless—schooling he might have persevered. I am even foolish enough to believe that I might found a school that can operate somewhat independently of the whims and willfulness of legislators who cut a million dollars from a school budget every time some unruly adolescent throws a rock through a "wrong" window; independently, too, of dancing hat in hand on the strings of a foundation official doling out someone else's money.

So, enough of the babbling. Let's dream a dream—a practical dream. From one who has talked of education as potentially poetic experience, practicality must sound like strange qualification indeed, but I immediately qualify the qualification by insisting on guidelines and components to be incorporated that were developed earlier in this quest.

I remember hearing the supervisor of a secretarial pool in the headquarters of a large corporation advising a group of teachers bluntly to get on with providing future secretaries with a sound fundamental education. "We can teach her in five minutes on the job how to run a mimeograph machine," he said of such a typical "vocational" or "business" high school course as Office Practice. Anyway, with the rapid changes in gadgetry today, the chances are that the machine she uses her first day will be obsolete before her fifth year on the job—if she stays that long. How many Americans learned the effective use of "sentence fragments"—not their rightness or wrongness, but their effective use—through reading Volkswagen advertisements rather than dutifully and diligently accepting the dictates of their thousands of English teachers? "Percentage" did not really get through to me until I first applied for time payments on a car, then more thoroughly when the first home mortgage came my way. In fact, what I had "understood" of percentage through my scholastic exposure to it hindered my understanding of the eventual reality.

It is obvious that a great deal of what the school now carries as its educational burden could be facilitated and accomplished by business and industry and government—by the "world out there," as kids usually put it. Can we go further with the statement and declare that far more education, overall, is accomplished outside school than in—more by maybe a zillionfold? At least tenfold, then?

One of "my boys" in the early days of my career haunts my thinking again and again. He had quit school on "working papers," then been laid off at the factory, and thus forced back into school by state law because of his age. I did not know he had been laid off the job, at first, and like the typical teacher I thought he had "seen the light" and come back voluntarily to "finish his education." (DON'T BE A FOOL—STAY IN SCHOOL!)

"Could you speak to your brother?" I asked Lew on his return. "He says that he wants to quit school, now, and I thought that since you've been out there and come back, he might listen to you quicker than to me."

"Well, I don't know if I could do that, Mr. Kline," came the reply, in a most benevolent and sincere way. "I wouldn't be back in here myself if I hadn't lost my job."

"But what about your education?"

"Mr. Kline, that was over in the fourth grade because I knew how to read, how to write, and how to figure by then, and that's all I'll need out of this school. I haven't learned much since then."

Lew was a good boy in class, gentleman, helper, participant, academically sound, though not outstanding, and he always had his homework done. I do not tell his story to claim that he was a broadly nor thoroughly nor deeply educated boy at sixteen—or in fourth grade, as he saw it. I do not bring it in here to argue that education should be strictly job training. Far from it! I only suspect that he might have made a more accurate observation than we are willing to make in two different directions: (1) What, basically, had the school taught him? (He himself reported the nineteenth-century American agrarian society's "three R s," you will notice.) (2) How much of his time in ten years of schooling had simply been "filled up" with something *called* education? To those two questions of his, I would add three more: (3) How much of what could he have learned outside of school during those years? (4) What are the fundamentals that are properly the school's to teach? (5) Just how could they be taught most economically and efficiently?

If we are to place service to individuals as top priority in the school (even as individuals need to be members of society), if we are to provide educational service that is "general" or "comprehensive" (that is, useful to all who come to the school), and if we are to operate that school according to the principles of economy and efficiency, it is obvious that we need to decide on answers to some of those questions. What is the school's job? What should it be doing—or can it do?

In planning my dream school, I hereby grant to business and industry, to hospitals, unions, government agencies, churches, museums, and so on, what they already carry in fact if not always in name: responsibility for most of the specialized education of the people which they need to maintain themselves as institutions and to grow as viable segments of society and economy and culture. The school will continue to provide certain services to that "outside world," as we shall see shortly, but it will no longer simply kill time with kids who can therefore be kept off the labor market that in large measure keeps the economy of that world somewhat in balance. It will no longer serve "society" at large at the expense of individuals in whom, after all, the personal element of humanity resides. Nor will it any longer pretend to that service to society which it has never been able to meet with any fully satisfying success at any rate: specialized training, especially for earning a living.

What criteria, then, do I suggest for "general" or "comprehensive" education such as that I would make the business of the school? The criteria are two in number: (1) What educational program or goal is the school peculiarly suited to meeting or carrying out in society? That is more or less the same as asking what educational needs are common among all individuals. (2) What educational tasks have not been picked up and carried out by elements of society other than the school—by business, industry, etc.—once they have been openly granted the jurisdiction and responsibility of those tasks?

Our inquiry has already thrown us toward my nominations for answers to question one. I quote from an earlier section: "... *unity, diversity, process,* and *substance.* They are all he needs to know (and, I suspect, all there is to know) to lead a full, rewarding life as an integrated individual within a human society."

Not very practical, I hear you say. All well and good, but not too specific! Fuzzy dream talk; cities are on fire! As foggy as expected of one who dreams of poetics in education. Mighty easily mouthed. "Talk Fahrenheit, talk Centigrade./Use language we can comprehend./Tell us what elements you blend."[2] I hear you now as always I have heard. How are you going to meet such goals? What will students do in your school? How are you going to organize your school on such a basis? Aren't we meeting such goals now? How will you know anyone's getting anywhere, especially since by implication of earlier evidence in your inquiry you have pretty well abolished time requirements and grading as components in meaningful measurement, overall?

Good questions. Further input needed. For now, a quick jump to relationships between "world out there" and school. My ideal

---

[2] From "Take Something like a Star," by Robert Frost, in *The Poetry of Robert Frost* edited by Edward Connery Lathem. Copyright 1923, 1928, 1934, 1949, © 1969 by Holt, Rinehart and Winston, Inc. Copyright 1951, © 1956, 1962 by Robert Frost. Reprinted by permission of Holt, Rinehart and Winston, Inc.

school system will provide a service to the world out there, over and above providing all persons who want it with a truly basic education in the fundamental structures of humanity as just listed. It will provide a brokerage service, a clearing house for matters educational. It will, for instance, gather, tabulate, analyze, collate, and disseminate continual data on the ebb and flow of needs and potential, of supply and demand, of overtaxed training facilities and underutilization of others in the various components of society that have assumed the role of specialized education to serve their own needs. It will become matchmaker for educational purposes, not employment agency or market analyst, but matchmaker. To return to our example of the office girl, let us suppose that an analysis by the school reveals that within a single metropolitan area, every two weeks twenty-five girls require instruction in the operation of, say, the spirit duplicator and the mimeograph. No matter by which company the girls are employed—they will usually be from a cross-section of participating firms in the community— the entire community knows that A. B. Dick or Bohn or Heyer or Standard can most readily instruct these girls in the proper use of spirit duplicators and mimeograph machines in just four hours. Fine. The school identifies that need, schedules the training session, notifies potential trainees—as economically and efficiently as possible. The girls spend less than a day learning something they need immediately; only one of the companies spends time and effort in the training, and the school needs to buy no machines, hire no instructors, force no kids to undergo training they might or might not need, stretch no simple learning project out over more than sufficient time for its accomplishment. Specific needs felt by specific individuals have been met economically and efficiently, with the educational institution serving as facilitator.

What about the competitive edge one company might gain over another in instructing people to use particular products? Won't other suppliers complain? Or, from another direction, why should one company bear the responsibility of training someone else's employees? A number of answers to such questions: If participating companies fear competitive edge available to the company selected to provide some specific training program, let all suppliers of that particular product or service or whatever offer training programs, and schedule each trainee for a session in each

different training program—even with a possible sacrifice of economy and efficiency, overall. (Have to keep the natives happy.)
However, in this age of standardization and interchangeable parts
and the like, I doubt that the training one company might provide
will differ substantially from the training its competitors might
provide. In fact, A. B. Dick, for instance, might invite its competitors to supply machines for use in the training program so that
trainees might get more comprehensive training in some specialty
plus an accurate picture of the total availability within the device
or field or whatever is the substance of the training program. Or,
if there is substantial difference, we obviously are not involved in
a problem of competition; rather we are involved in a separate kind
of program, and the solution to it is obvious: let every specialized
component of society assume responsibility for education in that
specialty in which it has accrued most expertise. Furthermore,
those units within the community not selected to provide one
particular educational service ought to rejoice that someone else
will pick up that task for them, just as various smaller airlines at
the present time send some of their employees to flight and main-
tenance schools operated by larger airlines, and smaller hospitals
depend on larger hospitals or specialized clinics to offer training
and to conduct research.

   One answer to the second question—why one company should
bear the responsibility of training another company's employees—
lies in the degree of specialization spread among the various participating units within society. That is, this "outside schooling"
educational task we are talking about might most economically and
efficiently be spread equally among the various non-school components of society, with every component assigning, say, one-
twentieth or one-tenth of its aggregate total of time and personnel
and resource to the total educational task of the community. (I
doubt if that high a proportion will be needed, once specialized
education, brokerage-style, is established.) In return for this direct
investment of time and other resources in the educational program
of the community, those participating non-school units of society
will receive, in addition to the service of more economically and
efficiently trained employees, a tremendous tax break—both for
themselves as companies, or whatever, and for their employees at
large—for the total school budget of the community will drop

tremendously once huge school buildings become less necessary (at least fewer in number), with a cutoff almost to nothing of mountainous inventories of hardware and supplies and materials within those buildings and a fantastic decrease in staffing, in the now ever-spiralling payrolls mandatory in each separate school as it tries desperately to bargain for specialized talent in sufficient quantity and quality to meet the total educational task now futilely expected of it.

To staff such a school service as the brokerage herein suggested for specialized education, what will be needed? Within a sizable community, a good computer, a coordinator or two, and a handful of clerical assistants. To make it possible, the will of the community and a frame of reference that allows us to set aside massive investments from the past—investments that infringe upon us more than they profit us, investments in sentiment and mindset as in buildings and books and bond issues. I hope that the various non-school segments of a responsible community will willingly accomplish all the aims and meet all the needs of specialized education—that is, educational needs not common among all individuals in society. If they do so, they eliminate the need for the second criterion named above for determining the business or purpose of the comprehensive school. In short, the school will not need to pick up any of the tasks of specialized education. If, however, some such specialized educational need is identified that absolutely no non-school component of society can be persuaded to meet, then I suppose the school will be seen equally irresponsible to society if it does not assume that specific educational task. But, again, economy and efficiency will be jeopardized overall, and the school will be pushed once again toward that impossible and horrendously expensive role of trying to serve as job trainer for 20,000 specialties. That way lies some of the fragmentation as well as stringency and strangulation, the empty iron shell, the impossible task that symbolize the dilemma of our present educational system.

Some thoughts, then, toward designing a school that will meet the first criterion suggested above: education in the structures of humanity, in elements common to all individuals in a society.

The Christ figure has long fascinated me—long after those early Sunday school days when I was told frightening stories, fairytale but ogre-like, about some carpenter's son who loved me and was therefore killed and how I am a sinner who is also, by some strange turn of logic I have rarely been capable of cutting into, somehow partly responsible for his crucifixion two thousand years ago. (A good example, I submit, of symbology that might have gotten in the way of sensibility over the centuries.) Part of the fascination lies in the paradoxes attributed to the teachings of Christ in the simultaneous simplicity and profundity of such statements as "Love the Lord thy God, and thy neighbor as thyself," or "Do unto others as you would have them do unto you," and that is all you need to know. But what lies in that word all? Twenty centuries of turmoil, massive cathedrals, miraculous statuary, martyrdom, wars, conquest, hospitals, suffering, acceptance, gilt and guilt—His own climbing of a cross.

When we as educators in the twentieth century ask what is it necessary to know in common with the rest of mankind, so many of us feel rather stupid even at daring to ask the question, and we are downright abashed to suggest any hint of an answer that would require less pagination than all the popular encyclopedia sets shelved volume to volume plus one copy of every book, film, recording, etc., that now exists. The crushing weight of the eventual product would seem to be the contemporary cross that would kill us all, such victims as we are of our data orientation.

Yet, one afternoon, three of us sat down to brainstorm an innovative curriculum that we might use in a workshop for experienced elementary teachers. We had been selected because one of us represented language, one social studies, one math-science. We had agreed, however, to develop a single curriculum, not the typical three- or four-part course of study representing equal time and space for each of those traditional categories.

Carl broke us open by hiding some object in a brown paper bag and shoving both into Michael's hands.

"Okay," Carl commanded, "you may not open the bag, but you may do anything else you want with it. Tell me what's inside!"

And, of course, with the bag between Mike and me, squeezing and smelling and shaking and poking and weighing and listening took place at a frantic pace—each minute action and reaction or tremulous suspicion analyzed and offered as a solution to the question of what was inside.

Carl, however, refused to respond with anything but more questions: "Are you sure? What makes you think so? How do you know? Anything else?"

Many readers will no doubt recognize the technique, for variations of it are in common use in various instructional approaches to curriculum throughout the country. But the point that the three of us reached with complete agreement surprisingly soon is that the exercise, led well by a competent instructor, almost guarantees that its participants will arrive at the concept of relativity, at tentativeness, at the recognition that perception is an act of an individual involving his organic capabilities and that reporting such perception is liable to all the error as well as communication that language affords.

Mike felt that if he could get all his pupils in the social studies to recognize that fact, he would accomplish one of his major goals in education. Somehow, some of his students would have begun to suspend actions based on absolute judgments.

"And, that's what I'm after in science," Carl agreed, "that students see science as a refinable process, a system developed by man and open to alteration as he looks out on his physical universe."

And, of course, that I believe such a concept is basic to the needs of humanity is evident, I hope, in earlier sections of this inquiry—those concerned overtly with language as process, at least.

The point is that I am sure we touched one of the fundamentals of human knowledge that afternoon—within perhaps two or three minutes of the start of the exercise. Let the supervisor of the corporation secretarial pool tell teachers to be about educating students in fundamentals, and he and most of the teachers think of spelling drills and comma rules and times tables—like unquestioningly memorizing words known as "The Seven Deadly Sins" without having the least notion what is fundamental to them, what they are all about. In fact, one might simultaneouly be gaily practicing every one of the sins, unaware they are what he has been ticking off rote-like as "shalt nots."

Whether "God is love" or "Tentativeness" or "Unity-Diversity-Process-Substance," the fundamentals of humanity—what comprehensive education should assume as its major province—do not require a five-foot shelf of books to identify, nor necessarily an eight- or twelve- or sixteen-year span of four- or five-month semesters to explore. If they are truly fundamental and if man is truly a creature capable of development within the single specimen known as "my life," they will be available to him for exploration in ever more sophistication of degree and example throughout his life. Furthermore, he himself—as an individual—will need to decide how thoroughly or extensively he recognizes any of those fundamentals from the windows of his own existence. He might gauge such measure, might gain perspective on his personal accomplishment through interaction with other human beings, but no one else can determine for him just where he is in his development.

Therefore, comprehensive schooling, as I design it in my dream, is pursued to the individual student's satisfaction; he determines when he has arrived at whatever level he thinks he has arrived at. As schoolman, I suggest that there *are* fundamentals of humanity, that there *are* basic concepts, but the learner decides ultimately what they are for him and when he has arrived at them to whatever degree he claims for himself. The school will be open to him no matter what his age, or his achievement or his lifeview.

I am pretty sure that given the definition of *fundamental* implicit above, there really are not that many fundamentals to be experienced or recognized by the learner. I hesitate to say *learned*, for I suspect that education as it is being dreamed here is more than ever before an "opening of eyes"—or, as I have phrased it throughout this book, a "heightened awareness of life." A few basic processes, a few basic concepts, a few fundamental skills, a few broad attitudes, offered through sufficient means in sufficient variety and sufficient depth to attract pluralistic individuals in a widely pluralistic society, will compose the entire inventory of a good comprehensive school. Data, as I indicated earlier, is readily available not only to the school but to anyone anywhere in society, and my dream school does not pretend to be custodian of data or repository for it. The problem of the individual in society today is not a dearth of data, for it is so readily available—indeed it deluges in to drown us every moment—that we can hardly escape it if we want to. The problem, rather, is the selection of data to meet our needs as private individuals and as members of society. Such selection is a matter of process that involves skills, and it is based on concepts and attitudes. If we are to offer a fundamental curriculum, it will have to do with such things as well as with the use of data. The library is the handmaiden of the world, not the cloistered property of the school.

In the name of economy and efficiency, no one need convince me that a good bit—maybe a huge majority—of an individual's *learning* of the fundamentals of humanity can be accomplished without the kind of institutionalized schooling that requires a school teacher in a school building facing people known as schoolchildren. In fact, I might argue—already have done so, I guess— that most of a person's learning now is accomplished outside school, and often in spite of school. Of course, the learning accomplished by raw and random experience tends often toward extravagance and wasted motion, so again in the name of economy and efficiency, let us develop the technological miracles already available to us, and let us continue to search for more. I certainly do not fear that educational television will make a nation of *blah* conformists if we can program Eldridge Cleaver and William Buckley in split-screen debate or that we will all be brainwashed by some subliminal hocus-pocus if we all of us as individuals retain the choice to turn off the receiver or switch the channel or give up the TV set for an alternate technological device in our immediate, specific, momentary, personal educational quest. (Of course, I assume a huge catalogue of technological devices and approaches and experiences and substances, etc., to be always available for selection by the individual learner at the moment of his felt need or curiosity or whatever motivation, if any.) Quite sarcastically, judging by the unimaginative use made of educational TV so far, and also of tape recordings, filmstrips, overhead transparencies, microfilm, and the rest, we have little to fear in technological overeffectiveness or "electronic domination" at any rate, for most of educational television to date has consisted of sticking a boring lecturer or a dry panel of two or three lecturers in front of a camera instead of in front of thirty or forty students in a lecture hall. When I welcome technology in my dream schooling, I welcome it with the assumption that we will begin to use it imaginatively. That again might mean taking it out of the hands of those identified by tradition as "educators" and putting it nearer the marketplace—or someplace where more of the action has been. I would hate to see what the typical teacher would do with Zeffirelli's fabulous film of *Romeo and Juliet*, and to watch any of most of the "Sunrise Schoolhouse" kinds of television programs—usually prepared by nearby universities and shown as public service by the local TV station—is to know exactly why they are often scheduled for "viewing" during such prime time as 5:30 to 6:00 in the morning. Perfect time for viewing—the dead hour for all swingers.

So, given imaginative development of effective home or neighborhood technological learning centers—voluntarily patronized—they could accomplish a huge portion of the "comprehensive" or "general" educational task in a community, and I include as centers such extravaganzas as some of the better expositions and trade demonstrations and the like of the past decade or two. The school, as an offshoot of its brokerage function, could program and maintain such centers, at least those not sponsored and maintained directly by other components of society, and could do so in response to demands from the learners who patronize them as well as from input received, analyzed, then reported by a research wing of the school. It is not impossible to consider a single coordination center in the nation that will administer and develop the entire home or neighborhood learning wing of the school system, although I suppose we might insist on two or three such centers in competition with each other so as to double-check against willful absolutism and domination of the wing by whatever maniacs or despots might happen into positions of leadership and then forget that the goal of the institution is to serve individuals rather than to control them. At any rate, I would hate to see every cowstop province in the country trying to maintain its own effective technological wing of "general education" in the fundamentals of humanity—and trying to do so economically. Can radio station WWWW in Left Elbow, New Kansakota, produce a show as technologically effective as NBC or CBS or ABC?

Perhaps much of the "specialized education" illustrated and named earlier might also be accomplished through such home or neighborhood learning centers geared as completely as possible to the uses of technological tools and devices—an educational automat, if you will, but free to anyone at any hour for the pushing of a button. However, I would want to see such specialized education conducted through such centers only if it could be accomplished more economically and efficiently than through the kind of approach suggested earlier. I suspect that such economy and efficiency might become evident in the less narrowly specialized specialties—in certain kinds of reading skills, for instance. (I am not convinced that all people must learn as many reading skills as possible, or even that all people must learn how to read, so I tentatively classify reading as "specialized education." Marshall McLuhan has not been talking simply about tomorrow; he has been talking about today, also.) Will I ever forget the first time I sat down to a keyboard for a computerized lesson in Greek word roots, and, with the slightest initial prompting from me, that crazy computer was responding to me by my name—"Sorry, Kline, you missed that one. The proper answer was *anthro*. Now, try this one. . . ." And, just think, had the mood for Greek word roots struck at midnight—or at two a.m. or five a.m.—I could have dialed in to that computer and received the same automatic courtesy! Let me try to satisfy such whim with Miss Grumpy at the other end of the line. That would be another kind of education.

So, what is it that is left for the school to do in education if it provides a series of brokerage services—some for educational offerings and experiences to be provided by technologically developed autolearning centers, voluntarily patronized? What man produces —specifically, his gadgets and machines, miracles and devices—can economically and efficiently free professional schoolmen for what is their unique task: those basic human skills and processes and techniques and impulses and stimuli and responses and actions and reactions which cannot economically, efficiently, *possibly* be provided by any of his products. I am certainly not about to lock horns with those science fiction (and not so fiction) devotees who see man on the horizon of transmuting his own molecular structures —within each individual, if we would have it so—to help us transcend all the traditional human limits of time and space and even form and substance that most of us not only take for granted but cannot conceptualize as being overcome. Were I to live to the year 2100, I would not be surprised if such a speculative possibility were to have become ordinary eventuality. After all, in his plans for overkill and ultimate weapons, whether by laser or plague or melting of the polar caps or all-consuming flash from the sky, man has only acknowledged that he has assumed capabilities formerly ascribed to the gods—total destruction of the human race. It remains now for man to assume the responsibility of the gods for creating and maintaining life and for allowing it some meaning, some reason for existence. That means to me that the more immediate problem for man is to survive the twentieth century, and I have, after all, by its title promised a "practical alternative" in this section of my quest. I can only assume that humanity as we know it is here to stay for at least a few years yet and that the best service we might perform in education is to establish a system that will allow us to survive the present as well as begin to accommodate whatever fantastic human future lies ahead—if any.

Exactly what those skills or processes or impulses are that distinguish man from his products, I feel no more qualified to suggest than most other people, but I have no doubt that together we could identify them—given time enough and will and openness and concentration. Some would have me say "group dynamics"; others "appreciation" or "interaction" or "aesthetics" or "sensitivity" or "Quaker community" or "self-actualization" or "psychotherapy" or "affectiveness" or "zen" or "pot" or any of all sorts of things. But I cannot be sure that any of those readily available answers finds me arriving at the satisfaction of my quest. I watch a colony of gerbils—organic, perceiving, non-linguistic animals— and they seem to get along without all that. Or kids on the playground—they somehow seem to get along just as clearly most of the time, yet they seem also to have something else going among them, this distinction of gerbil from child, of human from non-human. Arms around me in the night—that will do it, let me know I am more than animal. Or satisfaction at the accomplishment of a well-turned but hard-wrought sentence. Or the overwhelming wordlessness inside when I swing with Duke Ellington's jazz in a cathedral. Maybe this ultimate human component of my school should be one giant playground—for kids of all ages. Or a conversation with someone who will listen to me as no computer or automatic telephone answering device can ever do. Or a conversation in which I will listen to someone else. Or a conversation in which two or three of us arrive at an idea that neither of us had when we entered the conversation. As you probably know me from sharing this quest, I think I would have this human element of my school for "general education" concern itself basically with the analysis and discovery and exploration and handling of language.

But, more than anything else, pursuing this inquiry as an avowed pluralist, I would have this component of schooling—as economically and efficiently as possible—try to come as close as possible to being all things to all people. In short, I think I would have its program generated on demand and under constant regeneration. That would require system rather than substance, so I turn to a third kind of brokerage, plus a service in the uniquely and peculiarly human.

The catalog or program of offerings in my school of general education will be in continual development, and at least at the beginning, it will list hundreds of potentially educational experiences, resources, activities, modes of learning, approaches, suggestions, projects of a wide variety of sizes and shapes and lengths and values and weights. I can imagine anything from a ten-minute conversation with U Thant to a week's field trip to Williamsburg, Virginia, to an afternoon in Lincoln Park Zoo, to an hour in the Hadley Farm Museum, to a self-analysis inventory, to three weeks reading a particular book, to an hour's participation in a Roman Catholic Mass, to a talk session in a Mississippi Negro's shack or in a split-level in Scarsdale, New York, to a lecture by Buckminster Fuller, to a half-hour poetry reading by Robert Lowell, to a volleyball game, to a chess match, to a piano recital, to writing a song, to designing and decorating a home, to staring at a whirlpool, to dissecting a worm, to bouncing a ball, to collecting stones, to sensing different kinds of wind through different kinds of forests, to looking carefully at a face. As I have indicated, *my* decision as to what goes initially into that catalog will be simply those criteria listed in earlier passages in this section of my inquiry: for instance, that individuals as well as societies are incredibly, imponderably complex in their pluralism and diversity and flux and that an educational system should go as far as it can toward accommodating such pluralism, diversity, and flux; that any learning experience is welcomed for its own sake whatever its shape or dimension or vehicle; that unity of educational program will be found inside the individual who is learning, not in "courses of study" preconceived by people other than the individual learner; that the basic reason for the existence of a school as an educational institution is to serve individuals; that the primary reason for placing individual with individual in a school situation is that such human-to-human interaction should happen within the "school" component of education as I am dreaming it here, because such human-to-human interaction, carried out with intelligence and sensitivity, is the peculiarly human characteristic of social man. At the start, in my dream school, I will catalog those educational offerings that will most likely facilitate the recognition or experience—the *learning*—of unity, diversity, process, substance—the four fundamentals of humanity.

Any learner who comes to the school, whenever he comes and as often as he chooses, will fill out as many individual program requests from that catalog as he likes. Each request will be as specific as possible in naming the individual learner's desired resource (the person or book of film or whatever), his desired topic or concept or idea or area or hope or goal in the learning experience being requested, and the mode or technique or vehicle by which he hopes to accomplish that learning experience: lecture, discussion group of five, discussion group of fifteen, film, television, individual project, book, private conference, or the like. Similarly, anyone who thinks he has a learning experience to offer for general availability through the catalog will be encouraged to contribute it through this requesting process. Every day all such requests will be sorted, tabulated, analyzed, collated, and scheduled by computer, and the resulting educational program published a week or two in advance by whatever means are most economically and efficiently available for broadest informational coverage. Perhaps some requests will need to be held for later scheduling—if only one person requests participation in a group of five, for instance. Or perhaps that person could be shown those alternatives that come closest to meeting his particular request. Or some requests might best be met through the home or neighborhood technological autolearning center, and the learner will be so advised. I think here of a specified learning need that does not require person-to-person relationships, and that can be accomplished more economically and efficiently through the technological autolearning center. The point is that as closely as possible and as economically and efficiently as possible, the educational institution should be in service to individuals.

Now, if I am wrong in betting that the study of language (both *study* and *language* in their broadest senses, of course) offers the most fundamental "general education" in and for humanity, or if any other dreamer through a parallel model of educational utopia is wrong in whatever he nominates as general to all people, we must build into the system some means for correcting the error. What is human—uniquely and peculiarly human—should certainly manifest itself in the felt needs of human beings, especially if man's technology or if the other components of schooling as I have been envisioning it are taking care of less general needs felt by individuals—of certain job skills or of specialized training of whatever nature and to whatever purpose. Thus, specific requests not suggested in the catalog will be solicited at all times from patrons of the school. Such requests will be given treatment similar to the computerized process toward service I have just described for catalog requests. If my initial catalog is indeed erroneous in listing the felt needs of those individuals it was designed to serve, those individuals will by nature of the process available to them be able to shape the institution to meet those needs, rather than have to shape themselves to the contours and nonpersonal distortions of the institution.

To staff part of this "general education" wing of my school system, again we resort partly to a brokerage function, and that brokerage system will require, by the way, the first permanent section of school staff—those who will service and maintain computers. I foresee a need for "teacher" in the present typical sense of the word—an omniscient and omnipresent instructor—only if some person can be so identified by the sufficient requests for whatever service he uniquely provides to justify his full-time employment by the school. Ordinarily, I hope that everyone and everything in the entire community will be considered a potential "learning resource" and, again, that all members of the community make themselves available for whatever commitment in time and effort can be negotiated between school coordinator and individual citizen-resource. Such dream is not sheer wishful thinking when many citizens now would be happy to offer their schools an afternoon or evening a week in place of fifty or a hundred dollars of additional school tax money every year or two. Nor when business and industry are already gearing themselves to four-day weeks instead of five. Nor when so many people in general wonder how they might spend their additional leisure hours.

The various brokerage services—of requests from whatever direction, from those who think they have something to learn from the system and those who think they have something to contribute to it, and for whatever wing of the school, specialized non-school education, home or neighborhood educational automat, school for general education, and of resources both personal and nonpersonal —obviously require coordination, and so long as the computer remains the best facility by which to perform such a brokerage function, the school should hire those computer specialists and their assistants in whatever number and kind and quality are required to keep the system working economically and efficiently. I doubt very much that the payroll will come anywhere close to one-third the total institutional payroll in American education today.

In addition to brokerage services, by the way, before we leave them, the "computer people" will service whatever record-keeping might be requested by patrons of the entire school system. More about the record-keeping possibilities of the school later, but for now simply a note that computers again seem to be our most economical and efficient means of communicating masses and varieties of information such as the patron of this dream school system might accrue to his "credit" and want to indicate concisely to someone else—like a potential employer.

I would have a second kind of staff member—assigned specifically to service in the general education wing of the school system. Call this public but personal servant "advisor" or "warm, fuzzy thing" or "professional human being" or "counselor" or "guide" or "facilitator" of whatever you like, just so long as it means pragmatic believer in pluralism, lover of fellowman, clear thinker, and precise practitioner of language—that is, of humanity. Now somewhat wishful, I dream that these servants might be humanity's most intelligent, most educated people, as *intelligence* and *education* have been defined elsewhere in this book; that they might be highest in a heightened awareness of life and curiosity about it, experienced and happy and comfortable in the constant exchange of knowledge, perception, and beliefs, furthest in the personal development and aura and humility of wisdom, and that they will wish, but not mandate, the same for every other person.

Their duty is twofold: to serve as advisor and helper to any patron or learner who requests help, both in selecting from catalog offerings those items that ought to be requested by the individual if he is to meet the needs he has in sight and in channeling help or facilitating institutional service that might not seem available through the immediate school catalog. Second, to serve when needed in the human interaction or personal conference or listening capacity that I see at least initially as the unique role of the general education wing of the school system. In either role, I see the advisor volunteering perspective, suggesting alternatives in choice or point of view if not reinforcing choices or viewpoints initiated by the learner, recommending the enlargement or limitation or scope or number of self-assignments and self-expectations by the learner, or simply serving as a sounding board or more simply as a listening post. The advisor symbolizes and serves as the uniquely human element of general education as I dream it here. As such, he represents the presence or thrust by which a fellow man might discover himself or see himself in a way or shape or role different from that he realized the moment before.

The third sizable element of staffing in my dream school system, mentioned only in passing so far, will be a research wing, and I am thinking strictly of research that will deal directly and exclusively with analysis, modification, process, function, results, needs, etc., of the school system itself. Only as it services institutional education as outlined in these pages will it be serving society at large. I would not want it to develop a better typewriter for Remington or Royal or cheaper napalm for the Army unless that typewriter or that napalm made direct improvement in the educational service to individuals that has inspired this entire dream of mine. The research wing will have all phases of the total educational program under constant surveillance and analysis: requests, learning procedures, resources. It will hold economy and efficiency as criteria for technique and procedure, relevance and request as criteria for substance. Its personnel will include what we now sometimes think of as "philosophers" as well as what we now sometimes tend to identify as "rat psychologists," with a gamut of degree and variation between those two positions, for the research wing, I repeat, will recommend changes not only in the *how* of the program, but also in *what*. It will quite likely be from its analysis of specific program requests within the context of the total educational offering that the research wing will suggest what might be a likelier candidate for "fundamental to humanity" than "unity, diversity, process, substance." It will quite likely be the research wing that might offer a basic alternative to language as the foundation of humanity. It will almost surely be the research wing, working on the basis of request analysis, that will recommend increasing or decreasing frequency or duration of specific offerings within any phase of the total program, or altering the catalog, or modifying approach or technique or content in any offering, or judging relevance and measuring demand.

Each phase of the total program, I suppose—research, advisor, computer, resource, neighborhood center, specialized education, and general education—will require a chief coordinator, and I will add a moderator to keep them talking to each other as they mutually administer and maintain the ongoing school system.

So much for now of staffing, substance, system. But, how will the learner ever determine that he has "arrived"? Such chaos, I can hear you say. Obviously, it is now a fault of our system that our "measures" of schooling—diplomas, degrees, etc.—offer at best a foggy notion of the holder's education, and little more than nothing about his learning. Of course, as suggested earlier in this book, outline long ago replaced essence in our habit of certification, and many of us are in the remarkable position of trying to defend an institution that no longer accomplishes what it was instituted to do: communicate a person's abilities to someone else. We have two problems here: (1) How a person can be helped, if he needs such help, to see how far along he is in his education, and (2) How one person can communicate his abilities economically and efficiently, yet with sufficient depth and meaning, to another person.

First, if a learner needs a graphic indication or summary, however approximate, of his education or conscious learning, the school might establish with him an Approximation Index of Education for which he assumes major responsibility in maintaining, although the index itself should be filed at the school, especially as the information it carries might be "computerized" for easier storing and quicker transmission. I foresee a simple chart, and since I am accepting responsibility for this dream school, I take the prerogative to fill the blanks of the sample index with labels of my choice.

	Skill	Data	Concept	Attitude	Process	
Organic	U D	U D	U D	U D	U D	
	P S	P S	P S	P S	P S	_____
Perceptual	U D	U D	U D	U D	U D	
	P S	P S	P S	P S	P S	_____
Linguistic	U D	U D	U D	U D	U D	
	P S	P S	P S	P S	P S	_____
Post- linguistic	U D	U D	U D	U D	U D	
	P S	P S	P S	P S	P S	_____

U—Unity; D—Diversity; P—Process; S—Substance

Again, as I indicated in the fifth chapter of this inquiry, I realize a slippery quality, a certain shiftiness among the various categories reflected in the chart, and I am also quite aware of the great difficulty its use will present to those narrowly boxed-in people who have trouble deciding whether to put "fool's gold" under "fool" or under "gold" or to those who insist the obvious: that one man's foolishness is another man's fundamental. It is pluralism, after all, that I am trying to accommodate in all this. For myself, I could not care less which pigeonhole a person finally chooses so long as he thinks he knows why he has thus chosen. Neither does it bother me that there might appear to some people to be useless boxes or categories available on the chart. At the moment, I for one, for instance, am hard put to imagine a learning experience that I might record in the "U" box under "data" on the "Organic" level. That does not preclude someone else's seeing a very pregnant use for the category, however. I simply am satisfied that the chart allows everyone's using it, no matter what his personal lifeview or prejudice or poison or hangup or whatever. To encourage such comprehensive availability, you will notice blank spaces for that person who dreams of a universe not yet verbalized by anyone else.

How might such a personal report to oneself be used? Quite simply, whenever the learner recognizes that he has touched or identified or realized or freshly experienced one of the fundamentals of humanity (Unity or Diversity or Process or Substance) in one of the basic approaches to or purposes of his education (Skill or Data or Concept or Attitude or Process) on whatever level of personal sophistication in the particular experience or specific educational situation (Organic or Perceptual or Linguistic or Post-linguistic), he marks the appropriate block with an "X" or a check or whatever signal he chooses. Obviously, there would be value in making the chart three-dimensional so that he might pile up credits for himself in depth in one block, for instance. Or, the entire grid could be computerized, with various weights or intensities reported within various blocks or categories. The learner might substantiate his "crediting" himself in any one category by whatever means he chooses—by written report, or anecdote, or recording, or diary, or letter of recommendation, or chartreuse star, or autographed prize rubber duck. In fact, he might even choose to offer his personal Approximation Index of Education in support of his application for a job or in some other attempt to communicate to someone else what he sees as his general educational achievement. The other person might choose to pay attention to the index or not, might choose to request substantiation from the learner or not. (Remember, I suspect that a good many hiring-firing decisions already are made not with formal certification as the crucial factor. Often enough—too often—we use empty standards like degrees and diplomas to save us from interviewing in depth or from recognizing how terribly fallible we are in judging past experience, present capability, and future performance of fellow man. How often is the final decision of acceptance or rejection of fellow man based largely on emotional or intuitive or attitudinal criteria within us? How rarely is that ultimate decision based on certifiable data?)

A broadly educated person, then, will have checkered his index rather widely—with many different blocks marked off. A deeply educated person will, of course, have used the third dimension of the record—depth—to great measure. The narrowly educated person will have marked only a few blocks on his grid, and they might appear as a cluster. All the significant dimensions of general education will appear on the index—breadth, depth, shallowness, narrowness, concentration. If one knows that one lives in a society where skepticism abounds, one would be wise to have substantiation ready at hand for whatever his grid indicates—if he hopes to use his grid to communicate with others. If one hopes merely to provide himself with a picture to hang for his own satisfaction in the playroom or office, he need not worry about substantiation. If one needs no graphic illustration at all, he need bother with none.

(You might notice that I have omitted from the sample index one kind of curriculum I earlier developed at some length—the theme curriculum. I did so because it appears so much to be transition in degree between concept curriculum and attitude curriculum. It was more useful to me in that section to offer perspective on what we are now up to in traditional schools, whether or not we are aware of what we are up to.)

This reporting system—with other labels, obviously, in appropriate spaces—might easily be adapted to the sort of specialized education suggested above or to fields of specialized learning within any kind of curriculum. One individual might maintain a number of different kinds of grid index on himself, to meet several different purposes—one for his general education, perhaps, plus three or four for various specialized programs of education. The framework or structure of the device is what I hold more valuable than whatever labels I have stuffed it with for purposes of explanation here —although I myself would want those labels to outline the general education I envision. If you have followed this entire book through its development, you know that I have not chosen those labels for illustration haphazardly or entirely lightheartedly. They represent the comprehensive education I would have schooling provide. However, as an honest pluralist, I allow that others might hold different convictions or lifeviews from mine, and that even so, the device outlined here might be valuable to them.

Thus, you have the essential characteristics and components—at once simple, at once far-reaching—of my scheme for the ideal school system. It is more than a dream, now—it is a scheme, something I will be happy to develop in greater detail and seek to implement. I recognize many unsolved problems in this extensive utopian notion of mine—problems intrinsic to the scheme itself. For instance, I have no clear estimate of the effective scope of such mechanisms and organization as I have dreamed. Would home or neighborhood autolearning centers—fully automatic, offering incredibly wide varieties of learning experiences, technologically developed—operate best from a single nationwide control point, or would they better be organized regionally or within major metropolitan areas? How might they service rural areas or those wide open areas in the West? How many learners might a single school for general education, as described herein, be able to service most economically and efficiently? What is the ratio between number of advisors needed and number of learners or patrons to be served? How much learning can be indexed significantly by such a framework for reporting as an Approximation Index of Education? How many computers and how many clerical assistants would be needed to maintain the several computerized services suggested in the scheme? How large a catalog might a single school of general education offer to its patrons? What is the cutoff point between individual demands and the grouping required for economy and efficiency? I cannot guess clearly at the geographical limitations of the system or of its various components, nor do I have much focus on the limitations that availability of various kinds of resource might bring to the effectiveness of the total system. Cost details are very, very foggy in my mind, although I strongly suspect that cost overall would be a fraction of the total bill—public and private, local, state, national, specialized and general, endowed or tax-supported—now climbing each year in the United States.

I have toyed with the possibility that given the basic movement of this present inquiry of mine—from personal anger at abuses to benevolent scheme for alternatives—it is perhaps unwise to develop a system that will no longer get in the individual's way so much, that will serve and facilitate rather than control and frustrate, that will more nearly accept him where and how he is rather than reject and ignore him for being there. Perhaps we should purposely repress and deny and discourage so that creativity and freedom may more strongly rebound through riot—whether riot of art or of artillery depends on so many variables.

Such a thought brings to mind the teacher I heard of who could not keep his mouth shut in a classroom. Of course, he was unwilling or unable to admit that he was a compulsive gabber, so he rationalized his extremely annoying habit of talking to classes while they were taking his tests simply by claiming he was thus "teaching them to concentrate despite interruption and distraction." Rubbish!

Of course, one extension of this argument—that the repressed might rebound into richness and that repression is therefore ultimately a good thing—leads to absurdity. Yet, I have recognized, especially in the section on poetics, that genius and mystery and humanity and singularity might result from the interplay between system and egocentric thrust, between statement and framework for statement. Indeed, such belief leads me to seek this system I have dreamed rather than simply hope for some impossible openness, for some non-system, for educational anarchy. I am sure that in implementing the principles of economy and efficiency, even with the system I have dreamed, the negotiation necessary at various points to make the system work, the human-to-human components built into the school for general education and almost ensured in daily living, the natural drive for individual survival and for identity as an individual, and the basic human legacy of the race—to adventure into the unknown—provide tension and system enough by which the individual can mount his egocentric thrust and test his concept of himself as well as his prowess as a social being. Further, that they provide sufficient mechanism and framework within a total educational system not only to allow, but given the diversity available within the system, to encourage creativity.

There is no need for unnecessary institution to shove artificial barriers in the individual's way. The tension between his own skin and his schemes will suffice the fully functioning individual.

By similar argument, I do not see that the technological and mechanical aspects of my dream system—the "computerized economy and efficiency of it all"—will preclude any of the mystery or intuition or beauty or ecstasy or wonder or any other of the marvelous human attributes now personal and most sacred to men as they treasure and experience their sanctity as individual human beings. If economy and efficiency can provide whatever else is needed, man will be the freer to follow such impulses and to experience such heightened awareness of life. For economy and efficiency are not to be interpreted as educational austerity—not in the least. I would not strip Chartres of its stained glass simply because it is not easy to justify mundane function for it. How could I more economically and efficiently recognize one very important element of my humanity if I had no Chartres by which to recognize it within a breathless moment or two? How could Ghiberti have more economically and efficiently wrought his miraculous doors than by taking a lifetime at creating them?

So much for some of the unsolved problems within the dream itself. As we turn to a few of the questions raised from outside the dream, from the little worlds we now inhabit (I as narrowly as anyone else, I suppose), as we turn to such considerations, let me lay down one demand: If we are to consider this scheme in any serious way and certainly if any of us tries to implement it, let there be absolutely no unforced violation of ideal—absolutely none. And I offer three reasons why I would be so stubborn in adherence to the ideal. First, I have seen too many neat ideas slaughtered by improper or misguided or distorted or shortsighted implementation, then judged—for the wrong reasons—to have failed. It is not the fault of programmed learning as an educational concept that certain terrible "programmed" texts have been published or that certain teachers have completely misused some of the decent ones that are available. There has been no failure at all in the notion of computerized modular scheduling; rather, there have been misinterpretations and the like.

Second, for once I want to see us aim unwaveringly for the ideal. I am simply tired of people saying, "Well, we won't reach the ultimate, but at least the world will maybe have moved a half inch toward it for our efforts." I want to see education reach for the sun, for once, and either touch it or fail honestly and openly in the attempt. I am weary of meeting people at A, then preaching them C, so I can get them to B, maybe.

Finally, even if we fail to touch the sun, the uncluttered vision of the ideal, of the pure notion, will probably give me clearer perspective than we now have on what now is. If nothing else, such accomplishment will almost guarantee against that personal absolutism by which I can justify the destruction of my enemies— and by which they justify my destruction. And if we see ourselves falling so far short of the ideal that we are desperately beyond self-improvement, that we have nothing left to do but give up, maybe we ought to. I do not think mankind is at that hopeless point. In fact, much to the contrary.

Some will say that the alternative I have presented is not the practicality that I have promised in this quest. I think what they mean is that it does not seem immediately to fit within their boxes, it is not apparent from the little tunnels by which they view life. Or perhaps they mean that society could never adapt to such an educational system overnight, and I would certainly agree with that observation. It is not "practical" to abandon thousands of brick and steel school plants, many still in construction, nor to redefine the roles of two million educators, nor to toss huge inventories of supplies and materials to the surplus bins. Again, I agree, but I do not think "practicality" is what is at stake. There is nothing more "practical" than economy and efficiency. *Sentiment* is at stake, *memory* and *tradition* are being jarred and challenged, *investments* from the past are jeopardized. Yes, I agree with such observations, but do not charge my scheme with "impracticality."

There is a more realistic question concerning the "age of choice" and when an individual might reach it. I was tempted to list this question as one intrinsic to the scheme as outlined, but I am not sure that it is intrinsic. More simply, if schooling is to be voluntary and generated on public demand by individuals, how old will an individual need to be before he can make a conscious selection of program request? Will an advisor or parent or whoever need to select for a three-year-old, for instance? At first I thought so, but now I doubt it. It has struck me that infants probably do not know that they are "making a choice" when they waver between rattle and ting-a-ling, then pick up one or the other. I suspect that we invent whatever "age of choice" might exist when we force kids to realize that they may have one *or* the other, this but not that, or this *if* not that. At least at the start, I want sufficient variety and sufficient attractiveness of educational offerings—both in the home or neighborhood autolearning center and at the school for general education—that the natural impulses of the individual, however young or old, will be somewhat gratified by at least one offering at hand.

Many of the criticisms and questions raised about my dream reveal simply the difficulty many listeners or lookers-on have in developing a new and open frame of reference. Many people say *no* to an idea simply because they do not immediately see themselves or their schools as they now are, in the picture as education might be. They slap labels on portions of the dream, labels that smack of disapprobation or disbelief or of the occult or the faddist or the visionary. Or they say, "It's already been tried"—a statement I hardly believe, for nothing has ever been tried as it might be tried tomorrow. The existential moment is ever developing, and even if apparently identical phenomenon has been engineered and tried yesterday—with failure—the moment might be different for it tomorrow—to succeed.

Behaviorists identify "humanist" elements in my dream and curse it for those elements. Humanists identify "behaviorist" elements and curse the dream for those. So they wrangle or ignore the dream as a whole, or we dicker and dicker and dickory-dock, while 60,000,000 American kids sit passive or peevish in school, waiting for June so they—and their teachers—can get out—and gather sanity again. And 150,000,000 other Americans figure education is over for them because they have no red schoolhouse to have to sit in any longer.

Researchers tell me what is impossible about my dream and what can never work and how much of the dream is based on intuition and belief instead of empirical evidence, and I am almost nonplussed to get them to see that so much of what they tell me is of the past and therefore suspect, for it has been carried from within a frame of reference about people and things who existed within frames of reference that I might now want to ignore or alter. I will use what I can of what the researchers have learned, but I will not listen too attentively to their "reasons" why my dream school "cannot" work. I welcome their information and expertise and insist on their place in my new education, but I recognize, too, how often research has given us averages so that we have then tended to act as if all people are average, how Freud's late nineteenth-century psychological findings in repressive Vienna might not be so thoroughly applicable in late twentieth-century's go-go permissiveness of Miami or San Francisco or Las Vegas. I do not care that some statistical study indicates that most five-year-olds can recognize single vowels but not consonant blends if all five-year-olds are, because of that study, then required to work solely on single vowels to the exclusion of consonant blends.

So often, in seeing the educational world only from our own little boxes, we take a stand, "discover" a truth, and then spend the rest of our lives defending and protecting it.

As for those who have heard my dream and spotted "Multi-media" here and "Montessori" there and "Daily Demand" and "Voluntary School" and "Open Campus" and "Neighborhood Center" and "Computer-Assisted Instruction" and "Experience Orientation" and "Learning Package" and all the rest—saying that I would have us do only what others have already done or are doing or have suggested—I can say only that I have yet to go and see "it" being done and to come back *not* disappointed. I have seen school schedules generated on demand, yes—but usually by demand of the teachers, or, if by students, with such a put-up job of severely restricted choices that "demand generation" is not really getting a fair trial, for whatever reason. I have seen scores of very fascinating, very exciting elective programs—but very few voluntary ones, and then often as not carried out solely at the risk or personal investment of a dedicated professional or two and some kids—rarely with the total investment of the scholastic institution directly behind the efforts. I, too, have offered honest freedom of choice to students, only to be disappointed that they have made unimaginative, very ordinary choices, but I am not therefore ready to say that the idea of tremendous variety of free choice for learners is a bad idea. As with the orientation of research to data that is past, consider the huge weight of tradition and conditioning that have shaped the students we find in our schools today. Not half a year of first grade passes before most have realized that school has little to do with the reality of the world out there, rather that it is a game one plays so that one can get out at the appointed time. Or people show me a course "guaranteed" to meet the felt needs of the group, for the group has spent the first six weeks talking about what to talk about during the course. As one not given to endless conversation, I suggest that such an approach, while it looks awfully democratic, is far from pluralistic—and hardly economically and efficiently geared to individualization of learning. Let those who want to talk about what to talk about do so as long as they like. Let those who choose not to talk go down to the neighborhood autolearning center and press a button of their choosing or to the advisor at the school of general education and fill out a specified program request.

Euphemism, too, gives me its problems when I talk about my dream, for everyone can say, "Yes, my program is student-centered. That's why we're in business. You bet we believe in individualized instruction—why, every kid in class has his own copy of the textbook, and we give him the *responsibility* to go with it—(beamingly) to maintain it in good condition and (with an intimate, omniscient wink) to use it!" Talk about community involvement, and someone shoves you a PTA manual; education for every age, and they show you the ladies' evening woodworking class; neighborhood center, and you get the Saturday morning basketball league in the school gym.

At a workshop on salary and negotiations several years ago, we all agreed with the discussion leader, a top man in school finance for a national organization, that local property taxes as a major source of school revenue had about reached their maximum —that on a national average, the local property owner could hardly be expected to pay more. Seeking a new frame of reference, I asked if the organization had been considering alternative ways by which schools might be financed, but my question was taken as euphemism for "tapping the federal till," for the quick, smiling, confident answer was, "Oh, yes, we have a pretty strong lobby in Washington working on that problem right now." I do not see federal money as a significant alternative to local tax money when I happen to be the taxpayer supplying some of the money at both levels of government. I do submit that my dream might accommodate authentic alternatives when it allows barter for direct services to education rather than bond issues for more buildings, when it decreases need for mountains of concrete and steel beams and increases the likelihood of more efficient, more effective education for every individual as well as more satisfying utilization of talent now being misused in many of our very finest teachers and administrators, both those now in schools and not in schools.

I recognize that it is all but impossible for many people to remove *time* as a significant component in their thinking about education. We have been so long with six-year-olds in grade one and twelve years of free public schooling and Carnegie units and four years of college, and ten-month school years and fifty-minute periods that school just does not seem like school without them. We might better turn the observation around and say that school can hardly provide education economically and efficiently for every individual *with* them.

I recognize in my dream the sacrifice its implementation would require in our ties of sentiment and tradition to the past, to such habits as high school graduation exercises and valedictorians and Phi Beta Kappa and junior proms and class reunions and sheepskins. But I am sure that Kodak and Agfa and the other manufacturers will be able to dream up plenty of other uses of their film for us than to snap Junior's mortarboard leaning to windward. "School spirit" has long been a fiction—not nearly the reality in *esprit* that has developed in rock-and-roll fan clubs or in neighborhood gangs. Football teams can continue without school identification; they can continue openly for what they now are more often than not: business ventures for whatever or whoever sponsors them or subsidized thrills. The educational value inherent can be accommodated on demand through specialized schooling.

As for school boards and the whole issue of local "control" of education, I can hardly imagine with a mechanism so open as the one I have dreamed, with its responsiveness to the needs both of individuals and of society, with invitation to participate built into the system itself, that the question of control could come up. *Everyone* controls the school in the sense that it is shaped by individual request of whoever uses it or patronizes it. How any system can be more democratic or more conducive to pluralism I do not know.

I think I recognize all the problems that would be involved in trying to implement my scheme on any large scale, and I see them so forcefully that I am certain no one will want to try my scheme as outlined so far. Institution is by nature too conservative, society too prone to safety first. Probably that is the way it has to be, for now.

And I fully recognize the sanctity that past investment, however irrational or wasteful or stultifying, holds for some people. When mother has skimped on food and clothing for twenty-one years so she can watch daughter cross a platform in the hot June sun and take momentary hold of Prexy's hand while he gives her a college diploma, I could not want to destroy the need for such sacrifice within a year or two of its fruition. It would take at least a century, I suspect, before any such dream as mine could be given a fair trial, even though elements of it are operative today. But, overall, schools as are will survive—indeed prevail. After all, some of their practicing elements have survived centuries after specific need for those elements has disappeared or been superseded.

So, if we are to give any of the dream a good go in the immediate future, we need a nut or two to try it out, some experimental group of disciplined tinkerers who will serve as the advance patrol, as the safeguard society always demands, the first shaky dog on the thin ice of early winter. We need a little school, a pilot project, built along the model, as much as possible according to the framework, offering that most basic of all curricula—the language curriculum. (Might as well go the whole hog with my dream in this entirely practical proposal.) We need few personnel to get moving: several coordinators and advisors, some media specialists, a couple of hustlers and negotiators, a good couple of researchers (as defined in the dream), and some foolhardy questers who won't mind personalized education for the rest of their lives—or as long as they can take it.

Money should be no problem. Nonprofit and tax-free, we collect from the learners or patrons whatever financial contributions they can offer, and we establish a lucrative consultant service and lecture bureau. For society, while it likes to be safe itself, also likes to keep up with reports of the exotically successful or sensationally unsuccessful, either so it can leech or euphemize or borrow and adapt or gasp or pity or simply be entertained. We serve as educational missionaries to the surrounding community and take whatever falls into the collection plate for the cause. We might even tap any friends who will offer gifts with no strings.

If the ideas about education on which our activities are based are sound, if the dream is valuable, implementation will spread, notion will grow, impulses developed and tried, converts made, transition begun. Yet, even with built-in self-analysis and rectification, even with the capacity for continual modification of the program, we recognize that the effort could fail, that it indeed might not lead to establishing an institution that serves rather than controls, that helps every individual recognize his humanity, that explores with ever-increasing sophistication the unity, diversity, process, and substance of humanity, that economically and efficiently facilitates a heightened awareness of life and the development of wisdom through the exchange of whatever we have to exchange with each other.

What we need are a few people to try to live the dream, for a change. The saddest reaction I get to any of this is the unfinished utterance, "It's a wonderful dream, Lloyd, and I'd like to see it tried—I really would—but. . . ."

Epilogue

Language itself is humanity's ultimate, grand compromise—compromise between inner thought, unspoken truth, the wordless element of institution or impulse or faith and fellowship, verbal facility, communion with the rest of the human race. It is compromise, as I have so valiantly tried to illustrate in the passages about language in Chapters 5 and 6. This book does not really "say it all" anymore than the proposal for a model school "says it all"—for me or for anyone else. I have hoped only that the struggle for compromise might have resulted in coming closer to "saying it," closer to suggesting the ideal a little bit more precisely than ever before, so that the reader and I might come a little more clearly toward each other in dreaming an alternative to the present institution of education. I am quite aware that the compromise between that impossible dream, that ultimate quest, that notion or drive or vision just beyond language that keeps me always a dissatisfied man, the compromise between that and the book which we are now completing has developed in no small measure because of the struggle between impulse and words, between wordless statement and linguistic framework in which statement can be somewhat communicated—by hint or suggestion, at least. I suspect that that compromise is the same as the one that stands as entente between school structure and individual student, as poem between poet and poetic convention, as balance and vital tension between Individual and Institution.

I realize the extent to which language has shaped the thought that this book stands to reflect and communicate, and I am not an absolutist at all. Certain statements within the book have the trappings, the framework, the sound of absoluteness, but they are certainly not absolute in intent or in substance, however they might sound. As I said near the beginning of this inquiry, what sounds like statement from me is more likely the reflection of argument and dialogue that goes on within me most of the time. The statement I have made that is nearest to absolute in the entire book is my basic assumption that language is the basis of humanity, and even that one I can now rephrase to say more accurately (I think) that whatever man is in wordless truth we do not know, we can only at best believe—or feel, perhaps. Further, that language has made him to be whatever it is that he can talk about as "human" to himself and his fellows—including his reported perceptions of the physical universe. And, that my concerns and suggestions in this book have grown largely from such a view of man and his language and his humanity.

I know how incapable language has been at revealing and drawing out full impulse and notion through this book. It has been equally inept at providing the exact device to cage whatever thought has been revealed from word to word. But I think I have come as close as I can to gratifying both personal desires for now, and I hope the attempt has been as rewarding for you as it has been therapeutic for me—and, humbly and hopefully, that American education might somehow move ahead just a pace or two for the effort.

SONNET ON RARE ANIMALS[1]

Like deer rat-tat before we reach the clearing
I frighten what I brought you out to see,
Telling you who are tired by now of hearing
How there are five, how they take no fright of me.
I tried to point out fins inside the reef
Where the coral reef had turned the water dark;
The bathers kept the beach in half-belief
But would not swim and could not see the shark.
I have alarmed on your behalf and others'
Sauntering things galore.
It is this way with verse and animals
And love, that when you point you lose them all.

---

[1] Copyright 1951 by The Curtis Publishing Company. Reprinted from *The Open Sea and Other Poems*, by William Meredith, by permission of Alfred A. Knopf, Inc.

Startled or on a signal, what is rare
Is off before you have it anywhere.

William Meredith

Whatever rare animal might lurk beyond our quest, we know, even while participating in the linguistic exercise that is this book, that all symbols, including language, are negotiable and arbitrary. The fact that truth is forever unknown to humanity at large does not mean that we cannot communicate at all or that no man has his own personal vision of truth. But it does mean that every person indeed possesses and inhabits his own private universe to the extent that he cannot help but carry with him his own private version or dialect of the language he shares with fellowman. That dialect—I call it his own personal language—is distinct from every other man's. However feebly the model school structure proposed in this book tries to reflect that basic fact about the imponderable diversity of mankind, it certainly comes closer than the course-grade-diploma syndrome of the educational system presently in common use.